MINISTRY IN QUESTION

MINISTRY IN QUESTION
edited by
ALEC GILMORE

DARTON, LONGMAN & TODD
LONDON

First published in Great Britain in 1971
by Darton, Longman and Todd Limited
85 Gloucester Road, London SW7
© 1971 Alec Gilmore
Printed in Great Britain by
Cox and Wyman Limited
London, Reading and Fakenham

ISBN 0 232 51141 1

CONTENTS

Crisis in the Court Suburb   page   1
   Caryl Micklem

Servant of the Servants of God   page 28
   Neville Clark

Ministry in Ferment   page 53
   Ernest Marvin

Beyond the Crisis   page 78
   Alec Gilmore

CRISIS IN THE COURT SUBURB
by Caryl Micklem

It is difficult to believe now that Kensington ever went by that name, or that anyone could entitle a book 'Congregationalism in the Court Suburb' without raising a smile of indulgence or a hoot of derision. Yet it is less than ninety years since a memoir of Kensington Chapel, where I am now minister, was given that title in all modesty and seriousness (1). Today, although the name of the place still appears on the Court page of the newspaper, it is more likely to conjure up the museums than the palace (in fact part of the palace *is* a museum), and the suburban ring has long since expanded far to the west: but the sobriquet still serves to convey something of the nostalgia which haunts the stuccoed terraces with their proud window-mouldings – and also haunts the memories of some who still live there. One of my people has been in continuous membership with the same church since 1885.

The chapel is just off Kensington High Street, between the white commonwealth bed-sitter-land of Earl's Court and the fancy prices of Campden Hill, beyond which lies Notting Hill. Mansions of solid Edwardian flats have replaced the Victorian terraces on many blocks, and behind the bigger streets lie the mews, often with luxury conversions and penthouses above the rows upon rows of garage doors. It is a teeming, mostly affluent part of London. The average length of stay is three years. Very few of the people who regularly attend my church live within half a mile, except the children in the Sunday School (still so called), whose parents for the most part seldom come, even though the times of service and Sunday School coincide.

The building, erected in 1854 to seat eleven hundred, and regularly doing so for seventy years, has been modified inside so that sixty or so people do not feel too lost in it. It is a monument to a vanished age, when the trades and professions went to church with their families and their servants, when subtle class distinctions obtained between gallery and ground floor, and when the energies of the social conscience awakened by such men as Silvester Horne were poured into the running of a 'People's Hall' in the poorest part of Notting Dale.

It is that same People's Hall, now closed down and leased for commercial purposes, which makes it possible for Kensington Chapel to keep open, with a full-time minister and reasonably adequate upkeep of the fabric. The gifts of the congregation, which are generous, provide

1

for roughly two fifths of the annual expenditure.

What do we think we are doing there? Most obviously, perhaps, providing a battery-charging service for the 110 members, plus adherents, plus visitors (there are a lot of these, for the area bristles with hotels and Congregationalism is reasonably strong in North America and the Antipodes). They come because the worship is their kind of worship, because the preaching helps them, and, perhaps most of all, because the people they meet there, though extremely varied in background, education and occupation, share a sort of openness to ideas, a spiritual adventurousness, an esteem for one another's insights and a freedom from the shackles of tradition, which are on the rare side. Some, who once lived nearer, travel up to fifteen miles to come. The youth fellowship, with a number of students, graduates and young civil servants, is intellectually lively, though small, and like the church itself it fulfils a useful role in dispelling for its members the loneliness of the city.

When I came, in 1958, the People's Hall had just been leased, and the congregation was calling its first full-time minister since before the war. They were commendably open about their doubts. After fourteen years worshipping with a neighbouring presbyterian congregation, and four years back in their own church hall (rebuilt after a bomb), they had had to decide whether their continued existence as an independent group would be of use to any but themselves.

There was already the presbyterian church, scarcely more than a hundred yards away, and plenty of anglican churches of various hues, as well as the roman catholics who had rented our building while their bombed church was rebuilt.

The deciding factor was the Sunday School. No longer strong by its own pre-war standards, it was nevertheless still fairly numerous, well-staffed, and providing a service to the locality which it was felt must not lapse. That apart, the people considered that there was still a place for the kind of preaching (Bible-centred, expository, yet relevant to everyday affairs) which, rightly or wrongly, they believed that Congregationalism was well placed to offer to the neighbourhood. There was also the feeling that there could not be too many places of welcome and spiritual anchorage for the many people, often away from home for the first time, who were living in hostels and digs, studying or settling into their first jobs.

Five years, they reckoned, should show if they were right or wrong: and on that basis I came, having been for five and a half years in an

2

outer suburban growth-situation, and for four years before that in a group of country churches. At the end of five years, things had changed practically not at all. Many had left London, but just about as many had come to replace them. All the original considerations still held good. The Sunday School was keeping up. The private day school run by two members on our premises was providing an increasingly valued service to the neighbourhood. It was clear that many people whom we seldom saw were glad of our existence and in some sense supported by it.

Not, on the face of it, a crisis situation. Not a success story either: but, because of the particular sociological contours of our catchment area, we have just about held our ground for the decade and a bit. Yet from the inside it has felt like one perpetual crisis. At the end of each summer we have watched with bated breath to see if the new 'year' would bring new people, especially young people, to fill the gaps left by those who had gone away. Despite the financial security, we have been aware that at any moment it might suddenly become clear that the place was finished. Not that we have a large organisational superstructure to keep manned; there is a minimum of weeknight activities on church premises, for most of our people are committed up to the eyebrows in secular community service of one sort and another: but some leadership there has to be — in the youth fellowship and the Sunday School, as well as in the sheer running of the plant.

Within and beneath this continual and obvious uncertainty that underlies our outwardly even tenor, an uncertainty which I suppose has helped to keep us all more on our toes than we might otherwise have been, I have sensed the beginning and growth of new crisis-points. Baptisms are down. The small but steady stream of young people coming forward for full church membership (equivalent to confirmation, but usually somewhat later) has dried to a trickle. A bigger proportion of the youth fellowship (which meets at 8 p.m. on Sundays) is turning up after the service instead of coming to it first. Some of the most deeply concerned and thinking members find corporate worship meaning less and less to them.

With these I perceive also points of crisis in myself. *Honest to God* and all that has been profoundly unsettling as well as exhilarating. New translations of the Bible have forced me to face many questions about the preparation of worship, and prayer in particular. The rise and progress of local ecumenism, added to these theological and liturgical upheavals, has put paid to the old systematic instruction for church

3

membership which I used to give. What am I to say instead? I find that as often as not I feel impelled to spend the time carefully making hairline cracks of doubt in the smooth shell of childish belief inside which the catechumens reach me from the Sunday School nest. Doing it makes me feel intensely guilty: yet I cannot see them hatching into mature belief until it is done.

In other words, I am feeling on my own pulse the truth of some words of Geoffrey Ainger about the ministry as we have known it, 'We are witnessing the disappearance of a profession, but cannot bring ourselves to admit it' (2). If the sheep all start standing up on their hind legs wearing human faces and wielding crooks, that may be just what the shepherd has been praying and working for, but it is the end of him as a pastor all the same. He is no longer even, necessarily, the only theologically-trained consultant available to the lay groups upon which the task of worship-preparation increasingly devolves. In recent years I have usually had in the congregation at least one theological graduate who has not proceeded to ordination. (Another pointer, this, to the role-crisis of the ministry. They are interested in the subject, but cannot see what the job is.)

It is perhaps no wonder, in view of the winds blowing outside, that our denomination's doctrine of the ministry has so far remained tenaciously within its Reformation shell (itself the ill-adapted relic of days before most people could even read). Ordination and induction services are veritable banquets of atavism, at which, as Clifford Hill has written (3), 'it is part of traditional ritual for church and minister largely to ignore the processes of human selection and to describe their coming together as a pure act of divine guidance in which the mind of Christ has been revealed in the votes of the members'. Instead of just letting the man begin his job like anybody else, or at most saying, 'We liked him and he liked us, and so he's here', we maintain at this point a mode of speech, full of 'callings' and 'leadings' and 'receivings as from the Lord', which we should not now use at any other time, and which in fact we should think mischievous in any other context. Like dominical institution of the Lord's Supper, to which most of us continue to pay lip-service Sunday by Sunday although we know that it is at least highly debatable, this sort of language is retained to give a sense of occasion to what we are doing. If this were all, it would not perhaps matter very greatly. The trouble is that not only does this language represent what we do not really think, but its use wickedly inhibits us from saying to one another and to the world what we do

4

really think, and makes us liable to act in ways which our better judgment tells us are inappropriate.

For example, even quite mature Christians, who have long outgrown the belief that God pulls strings behind the scenes, are wont to say, when their plans are going well, 'I can't help feeling that the hand of the Lord is in it'. Harmless enough? But the moment this has been thought it becomes, as it were, the substantive motion and a new set of standing orders applies, From now on, the normal canons of judgment about those plans are wholly or partly suspended. The planner himself can no longer look at them on their merits; and would-be critics are silenced before they begin. Yet in truth the proposition, 'It is going well, therefore it must be right', is utterly superstitious and sub-christian.

Similarly, when a new minister is asked, 'Do you believe in your heart that God has called you to this ministry and to this place?' or words to that effect, usually several times, and the congregation is asked, 'Do you receive him as from the Lord?' a comparably mischievous inhibition of ordinary human judgment is demanded. It is as if the people said, 'We will listen to what he tells us without using our critical faculties, because the Lord has sent him'. Fortunately, they will do nothing of the sort: but if they took his induction service at its face value they might. Again, I have heard otherwise reasonable men state that it is at the moment when the ordination prayer is offered that the ordinand actually becomes a minister, for 'something happens to him then'. And if I have expressed polite scepticism it has been met with the half-shocked and half-pitying reply, 'Would you deny to God the prerogative of answering his people's prayers?' Yet those same prayers, if analysed, usually turn out to be requests to God to grant to his servant a number of gifts and graces, without the prior possession of which the man would never have got past the candidates committee, let alone received a call from a congregation.

It is the same with 'believing in one's heart that God has called one'. Layer upon layer of time-honoured misapprehension veils the issues here. First, there is the assumption that the primitive and highly pictorialised categories of burning bush and 'O give me Samuel's ear' form the only authentic way of talking about the Holy Spirit's motions in the human heart. It is call or nothing. Second, there is the implication that God calls people to the ministry because the ministry is especially God's job – a notion which ought to be repugnant to Congregationalists of all people. And third, there are the sad and

5

unedifying hypocrisies that spring from trying to speak of a straightforward human transaction as if it had taken place in another world altogether, a rarefied place where likes and dislikes play no part – or only a shameful part. 'How can he say it was God's call,' one hears it objected, 'when everyone knows it was his children's schooling that brought him here?' And the inference intended to be drawn is that he ought not to have considered the children, but ought to make himself available to go where God wants him to go, regardless of things like that.

But how does a man discover where God wants him to go regardless of things like that? His circumstances, background, temperament are all essential clues to the discovery. Even if the decision to move were not his, and he were simply directed, these things would be considered by the directors. Why, then, admit these but exclude other of his attributes which are now just as much a part of him as his academic bent or common touch – his possession, for instance, of a wife who dislikes the draughty parsonage at Exton, or a bunch of children for whom a move to Wybury would mean a serious slump in educational opportunity? 'Because,' I suppose someone might rejoin, 'the willingness to make sacrifices is one of the marks by which we recognise a true call to the ministry.' Why just the ministry? It is one of the marks of christian discipleship. Why in the case of the ministry should we set ourselves up as judges of what is and what is not sacrifice, when in relation, say, to the weekly giving of our fellow church members we are scrupulous to avoid doing any such thing?

One answer might be that we are really thinking about the ministry in the same way as those who argue for celibacy. We reject their conclusion but accept their terms and try to apply them to families. But the terms must be rejected as well as the conclusion: for all who profess christian belief are in the task of ministry together. Those with special gifts and training use them 'to equip God's people for the work of ministry' (Ephesians 4:12). There is no more reason to talk of God calling the equippers than the equipped; and although 'calling' is one of the characteristic New Testament descriptions of what makes a man a Christian, we do not, as a matter of fact, use it when receiving people into full church membership. We say instead, 'Do you believe in . . . ?' and, 'Do you promise that . . . ?' So with entering the ministry or moving within it. We become convinced; and our conviction is rightly subjected to the test of our fellow Christians' judgment. It is the more important, then, that our conviction should remain within the area of

6

normal criticism, and not be lifted out of that area by pious circumlocution on to ground where we cannot say anything without setting ourselves the absurd and impossible task of measuring the God-factor in a man's heart and mind.

I have dwelt at some length on this one matter partly because I believe it exposes some of the inconsistencies, if not flat contradictions, in the Congregational view of the full-time ministry — inconsistencies which must be recognised and eliminated before we can take any useful steps towards the new pattern of the corporate ministry of Christians in a place; and partly also because it is a good example of the tendency to 'resacralise' the things we do together. Since the closing of the credibility-gap between the gospel and modern man depends to a great extent, in my judgment, upon our ability to halt and reverse this tendency, I turn now to consider some of its other manifestations.

THE SUPPER

Many will remember, from the well-known parody of the even better-known ballad, the lines, 'What did you do there, Henry, my son?' 'Eat, dear Mother . . .' Henry had evidently not been to church. Not to the main church building, that is. He had possibly been to a harvest supper or a sale of work; but not to a service. Yet the central, the characteristic, act of christian worship is usually called by Congregationalists 'the Lord's Supper'.

The moment we have said it we begin to shy away from it. 'The Lord's Supper will be observed next Sunday,' we say. But to observe a supper is no way to treat it, surely? 'Ah no, but, you see, it is the Lord's commandment that we observe.' I have referred above, and shall refer again below, to the question of how far it is proper or useful to claim liturgically a dominical authority which we doubt academically. Here I am concerned to notice that we would rather fasten upon any secondary aspect of the occasion than its obvious and primary one of being a meal. 'The sacrament of the Lord's Supper will be administered . . . celebrated . . .' but never by any chance 'eaten'.

I know that in this refusal Congregationalists are in the main stream of christian tradition, and that the stream has been flowing in this direction for many centuries, perhaps ever since the baneful effect of men's lower natures began to make the early Christians' love-feasts come out in 'spots' (Jude 12). But we do not now reckon that the number of centuries during which mainstream christian thought believed the earth to be flat and creation to have taken place in six days

7

has much to do with what it is right for Christians to believe today. My contention is that what I shall call the 'sanctuarisation' of the Lord's Supper is a primary symptom of a disease which has attacked all parts of our body corporate, and which is likely to prove far more deadly to our mission than a few of Jude's spots, should they recur.

Writers such as Harvey Cox (*The Secular City*, ch.1) and Lesslie Newbigin (*A Faith For This One World?*, ditto) have shown convincingly that it is the faith of the Bible that has been chiefly responsible for the secularisation of western thought. The creation stories in Genesis desacralise nature, giving to man the freedom of it, so that he can explore it without fear that he is profaning what is not his. Upon this assurance the whole of modern science and technology have depended. Cox argues that what Genesis does for nature, the Exodus does for politics, and the covenant at Sinai does for human values.

If this is the case, then any movement in the opposite direction, back towards a supposedly 'sacred' sector of experience or concern, is a movement against the whole tendency and pressure of the Bible. This holds good for religion no less than for nature, politics and values. To live within the revelation Christ has brought is to experience the desacralisation and desanctuarisation of worship, of holy places, of sacred times. This is the clear testimony not only of the Fourth Gospel, with its 'neither on this mountain nor in Jerusalem' (John 4:21), but also of Acts, with its breaking of bread in one another's houses (2:46), and its 'Rise, Peter, kill and eat' (10:13). Between clean and unclean foods, between the holy nation and outsiders, between sacred contexts and secular, the barriers are seen coming down all over the New Testament.

Yet in the christian religion as we know it they are mostly up again. Not along exactly the same lines, it is true, but near enough. Churches which are for all practical purposes segregated by class if not by race. A Sunday which in Scotland and far beyond has become 'the Sabbath'. Feasts and fasts, vigils and devotions – these are for very many Christians an essential part of the 'method' of their discipleship. And all centred on the church building, the separated structure. Into it we 'withdraw' or 'turn aside' from the cares and busyness, the comradeships and solitudes, of the 'everyday' world. 'Lo, God is here,' we sing, as if Jacob's ladder had been marble steps under a gothic vault; when what that dream really represented, evidently, was Jacob's heart-stopping realisation that God is not tied to his altars, but fully operative even in otherwise god-forsaken places like Luz. Free Church
8

buildings (though frequently called 'Bethel') do not, on the whole, carry as noticeable a burden of the numinous as do those which stem from, and are devoted to, a more picturesque tradition of worship: but for those who regularly attend them, and for whom they thus acquire a beauty not always obvious to the eye of the casual beholder, they represent as definite and indispensable a devotional focus as any priestly shrine. People develop for them a fierce, proud loyalty which has bedevilled countless redeployment plans and union negotiations.

It is the same with the atmosphere and ordering of acts of worship, and above all with the details of the way we do the Lord's Supper. By 'we' I mean any one local congregation. The precise details will vary quite considerably from congregation to congregation; but never, or hardly ever, from occasion to occasion in the same congregation. Matter-of-fact though it may consider itself to be, and implacably opposed to all forms of 'bowing and scraping', a Free Church congregation will in fact celebrate according to a precise ritual, formal and invariable. Worshippers may even have to move into alternate pews, so that the quiet-soled elder or deacon may pass along and serve each one, and so deliver him from the need to entertain for a moment the distraction of his neighbour's existence.

In other words, reverence has as nearly destroyed the eucharist with us as with anyone else. And because it is all done under the aegis of the New Testament 'warrant', the dominical institution, our own manner of doing it acquires in our eyes, from this very fact, a spurious given-ness. It is for us as if Jesus himself handed round, in the original upper room, little crustless cubes of white bread on a silver salver. A piece of bun on a board, or a pile of sandwiches on a china plate, would seem all wrong, have all the wrong associations.

It is not that I think associations unimportant, or that I wish to beg any questions about whether or not the eucharist is in fact the Lord's 'own appointed way' of coming to meet us. I am simply concerned to suggest that we have made the whole thing too sacred — so sacred that we have practically lost it. And if instead of saying, 'The Lord did this and so we must do it,' we were content to pitch our tune a bit lower and say simply, 'Eating and drinking together has been the characteristic act of the christian community from the beginning,' I think we should have taken a decisive step towards a worship that celebrated and included the world instead of turning its back on it.

There are, after all, enough reasons in the jewish background and context of the first christian communities why a fellowship-meal should have been characteristic, without adducing an 'institution in perpetuity' on the part of Jesus. No doubt such a notion has helped to ensure that the institution has been perpetuated. But it is also this same notion which has permitted such a high degree of ritualisation to occur: and that, I argue, is a great loss. The Jews have managed to avoid this. Passover, like eucharist, claims the authority of perpetual injunction: but it is still a meal — involving family, neighbours, relationships. For all its sacred associations it remains recognisably something one might do with one's friends — sit down and have dinner.

Not so the eucharist. As a 'divinely ordained' sacrament, administered by a 'divinely ordained' priesthood or ministry, it has moved off into the sanctuary in such a way that it is now only the sacred significance that keeps it going. No one would dream of doing in ordinary life what we do at the Lord's table. This is just as true of the Free Church way as of any other. Any host who took to offering his guests a single minute cube of dry bread, followed by a thimbleful of liquid out of a bottle clearly marked 'Not To Be Used As A Beverage', would soon find acceptances to his invitations falling off as dramatically as church attendance.

The growing practice of celebration in houses shows up in a particularly glaring way the incongruity of what has happened. Use the kitchen table, and at once the kitchen gets transformed into a para-church. The table is cleared of everything but the sacred vessels; there is a reverent hush as people struggle to get 'atmosphere'; and then, as likely as not, the formal cadences and exchanges of liturgical language. Such occasions can be moving and impressive, but they illustrate as well as anything could how sanctuarised our approach to worship has become. The house has turned temporarily into a church; when the eucharist has gone away it will be able to revert to being a house again. Few things are more eloquent of the sorry divorce between religion and life than the spectacle of people, together in a living-room arranged for conversation and community, solemnly turning their backs on each other in order to kneel against their chairs and pray.

If arrangement and language were all of the trouble, there would not be too much to worry about. More appropriate styles would be found as people got more used to the house-context. But in fact it is precisely the sanctuarisedness of worship in general and the sacraments in particular that people most value. Your true-blue Free Churchman may be in theory opposed to the whole notion of sanctuary; he may claim

10

with Cowper that 'every place is hallowed ground' (though more likely he will behave as though no place is hallowed ground, and dump his hat and coat on the communion table to drive home his point): but try doing the eucharist a little differently, or suggest that the youth fellowship should celebrate as well as conducting the rest of the service, and you will quickly discover that what the man really wants is the magic as before, handed out in a properly authenticated way by the resident magician. Amid all the contemporary uncertainties in worship — which translation shall we use?, which interpretation shall we give?, in what terms shall we celebrate our faith and pray for our neighbour? — he is more than content to rest assured that there is still one way, one part of worship, in which the coming of Christ to his heart can be devised and pre-empted.

'His heart', singular. I do not mean that he is selfish about it. Christ will come to other people's hearts too, no doubt. But one by one. The fruit of sanctuarisation is individualisation. Something special is happening in there which each comes to avail himself of. The Free Churchman does not speak of 'making his communion', that deplorable anglican usage, but his approach is quite as individual as that which the usage implies, and everything he finds when he gets to church reinforces it. The diced, already-broken bread. The individual, already-filled glasses. The fact that he need not even go up and kneel beside someone else but may if he chooses receive the bread and wine in splendid isolation, and indeed is encouraged by the reverent atmosphere to shut out as far as possible all thoughts of other people. The liturgists may — indeed they must — go on, until they are blue in the face, about the corporate nature of the eucharist: to the man in the pew (that harangue-orientated, anti-encounter, inflexible pew) the eucharist has long since ceased to be an occasion primarily of fellowship at all. It is the individual's hot line to grace. Can anyone be surprised that many people find offensive our implicit claim to possess such a line, and refuse to have anything to do with it? I do not believe that this is part of the necessary offence of the gospel. I look in hope towards every move and experiment which makes the eucharist-meal more realistic and less stylised, more shared and less distributed, more inclusive and less exclusive, more open-eyed and less devotional, more domestic and less ecclesiastical. Although, as I shall argue in my closing paragraphs, there will always be a place for 'crowd'-occasions in christian worship, I do not see how the eucharist can be the heart and focus of these without turning into the thing I believe it ought not to be be — a piece

11

of hieratic, distance-enchanted magic. The whole concept of the eucharist as the central 'church' service needs to be questioned, unless indeed one believes that the function of the eucharist, and the primary task of the church, is to be for ever appeasing the righteous wrath of the Father by continually reproducing the Son's self-offering.

That sort of theology is not for me, and I do not in any heart-felt way recognise it as christian. The fact, to which I shall turn in a moment, that it is far closer than my own to what the psychologists tell us that people want from their religion if they are going to be religious at all, simply strengthens my attachment to the idea of religionless Christianity. It also, of course, deepens my personal role-crisis as a professional in religion.

Before coming on to that, however, I mention two further consequences or outworkings of the sanctuarisation of which I have spoken. The first is that the magical expectations to which it gives rise cast their shadow not only over the eucharist and (as I indicated earlier) the ministry, but over everything else that happens in and around church. Those who do not feel a need for religion (and Christianity is as much for them as for the others) see perpetuated in our buildings, in their arrangement and contents, a view of christian discipleship and nourishment which contributes to their rejection of all we have to say. To them these things look like part of an elaborate system for getting God organised and tamed and in men's pockets. Are they wrong to want none of it?

The other unfortunate outworking of sanctuarisation is in the attitude of Christians to the world around them. A sanctuary-centred piety distorts everything it sees. The huge complexities of the modern world are shrivelled and simplified down to the question of whether people come to church or not. If they did, everything would be all right. Since they do not, everything that is wrong must be their fault. A parody and an overstatement, yes, but not by much. We do have the propensity for describing experience in a particular way and imagining that by doing so we have disposed of it. If it fits, take it in: if it does not, send it away, like a scapegoat, bearing all the blame. Consider, for example, two extracts from adjacent articles by churchmen in my local paper.

'Though these are days in which great strides are being made in science and technology and . . . education, they seem to be discouraging days for the church. Though we preach the gospel of

12

love and humility so few people come to listen to us. Though we pray for a world to be saved from fear, suspicion and lies all these things still go on . . . How can all this be changed? A rededication and a christian education are needed. Let us teach the faith with energy and conviction.'

Not a hint that we must come out and face and study the problems. Simply get back into the sanctuary to rededicate ourselves and climb into the pulpit once again.

In the next column is an article on loneliness – a major problem in this area. Says the spokesman of the church,

'After forty years of experience of this problem I have become absolutely certain that its solution is being sought in the wrong direction. Loneliness is basically a spiritual and mental condition and really nothing to do with how many people are around one or whether one is rich or poor. It is rather the inevitable consequence of becoming an egoist, that is a self-centred, self-opinionated, selfish person'.

Given that there is a grain of truth in both extracts, they nevertheless present an almost incredibly smug picture of the sanctuarised church, taking it completely for granted that *it* is in the right place and all that needs to happen is for others to see some sense. 'People are to blame for their own loneliness! (It's not our fault.) The world is hard-hearted and proud so of course it comes to grief! (It's not our fault.)' I should judge these two articles to be fairly typical of what local churches are heard to be saying to the people of their locality. From outside, it sounds like an endless, bitter whine of, 'The world owes us full pews'. If this is a ministry to the world, then roll on the crisis for it! Its gospel has become sanctuarised, pietised, interiorised, almost beyond earthly recognition.

THE WORLD AND WORSHIP

But what if people love to have it so? It could plausibly be claimed that the reason why the churches are so thinly supported is that they never arrive on the scene until people are just leaving there and going somewhere else. For a century they have been dismissed as perpetuators of superstition by a public that believed it had been liberated from that mist into the clear air of science, both natural and social. What the public did not know (and most churchgoers did not know it either) was

13

that all this time a comparable revolution was taking place in theology. Biblical criticism and archaeology were transforming our approach to our sacred writings, while philosophy, sociology and psychology were transforming our approach to doctrinal formulations, ecclesiastical organisations and cultic activities. And now, just when we seem to be beginning to discover ways of doing theology, and church structure, and worship, which a genuinely contemporary man can honestly engage in without selling his birthright as a liberated person, a son come of age, we find the psychologists telling us that we are quite on the wrong tack again. People, they say, have their fill of the contemporary and the rational in their everyday lives. If they come to church, they do not wish to be expected to be contemporary and rational there too. They want mystery, *mana,* something occult and a little frightening, something to make them feel aware of a world other than this one. The figure of the 'man for others' has nothing for them: myth, miracle and magic are what they want to swallow.

Faced with such frowardness, what are the churches to do? Are they to run after the public once more, saying, 'But we have what you want! Here are your miracles, even demons if you like; here are mysteries and secrets and initiations in plenty; books full of strange language and ancient wisdom which mean one thing to an ordinary reader and another thing to someone who has been duly instructed; ritual to admit you to a world barred to the profane'? Or, alternatively, are they to say, 'This race to keep up with the world is unseemly and inappropriate. The proper study of the church is the worship of almighty God, and there is no reason whatever why the world should write the agenda for that'?

Honesty deters us from adopting the first alternative — as a deliberate policy, that is. It may be that those sections of the church in which mystery and miracle are given most place will gain some numerical strength from the new swing of the pendulum; but probably not for long, for here too *aggiornamento* has irreversibly set in. The transformation which has come over theology is a genuine transformation, not a trimming to keep in line with secular fashion. Even if the higher criticism was triggered off as a reaction to Darwin, it was never, as some would have us believe, an attempt to sell the pass to the enemies of the gospel on the most profitable terms. The movement of christian thought has had, and has, its own integrity, and it is unthinkable that we should turn aside from the quest which that integrity demands in order to court popularity by flourishing a new
14

obscurantism.

On the other hand, it is equally impossible for us to be content to say that theology and worship are concerned with 'another world', and that therefore their integrity is self-contained and need not trouble itself with questions of relevance to the climate of modern thought. If the christian God were all transcendence, and if christian worship were all adoration, such manichean dualism, constantly urged upon us by Malcolm Muggeridge, might be a live option. As it is, the incarnation requires of those who believe in it the continuing confidence that God is in the world, that he belongs there and is to be found there, not merely encapsulated in an ethereal bubble, a strange visitor in a diving-bell on the ocean floor, out of his element, unattainable by those who live there unless they have the key of the air-lock and so pass out of *their* element. If the glass breaks, that God is dead. But that God is not the God of the New Testament. Christ's descent 'to the lowest level, down to the very earth' (Ephesians 4:9) was accomplished without breathing apparatus. He was one of us, and in his coming gave gifts to men, the possibility of 'mature manhood, measured by nothing less than the full stature of Christ' (ibid., vv.8,13). Christian worship, therefore, is not all adoration, but also comprises hope and expectation for man — for the worshippers themselves, and for the world in which they live and which their worship impels them to serve.

That being so, it is important that the mental diagrams which worshippers form about what is happening when they pray shall bear a recognisable resemblance to the diagrams which they form about their everyday relationships and attitudes. Does God take action, in the way that governments take action, setting in train specific chains of cause and effect which at some point include ourselves, our friends, and other groups for which we may feel concern? What religion appears to say about this is so different from what common sense says that most people now feel it is a question of choosing between them. Hence, in part, that 'crisis of worship' everywhere which the 1968 Assembly of the World Council of Churches at Uppsala noted at the beginning of its report on the subject.

Since the preparation and conduct of worship occupies a large part of the time and attention of those who are whole-time or part-time ministers in the churches, the crisis in worship is a prime constituent of the crisis in ministry. In traditions where the task of the minister is to lead the people through a liturgy whose prayers are framed within the context of an obsolete cosmography, this is perhaps felt principally as part of the crisis of authority. The reading of the liturgy is part of the minister's obedience; official reforms are slow and leave the real issues untouched: what is he to do? Private conviction and public performance must somehow hobble along on different levels.

Yet his case is perhaps less critical than that of his Free Church colleague, who is responsible for the content of the prayers he leads. If he chooses prayers from a book, he must do so believing that they best represent the prayers of his people, or at least that they do so adequately. If he prepares his own, he must soon begin to face (unless he is a glutton for pastiche) questions not simply of contemporary language as against the imitation jacobean which has up till now held sway in the courts of the God of the Authorised Version, but also of metaphorical stance, of the appropriate direction of address as well as its style, and indeed of the shape and presuppositions of the whole cultic act.

To face such questions is frightening, because one has the feeling that once they are admitted to one's thinking one may find oneself, in the short term, unable to say or do anything when it comes to eleven o'clock next Sunday morning, and, in the long term, one may become bereft not only of the accidents but also of the substance of religion – *intellectus quaerens fidem.* I have found, in talking about these questions with fellow-ministers, that while some respond with alacrity and gratitude to the opening up of the issues, others whom one might expect to do so, since for the most part they are open and progressive in their thinking, react with fierce hostility to the suggestion that the traditional account of prayer may no longer be adequate. It is as if they felt that even to admit the possibility might be fatal to their whole position. I fully sympathise with them, having had – and in a way still having – the same feeling myself. Yet I am convinced that there is here a hurdle which must be surmounted, not refused, however great the crisis of self-confidence which must be gone through during the run up. People must face their own misgivings in their own way: the ground in which one man finds some signs of an answer will not be the only way forward. Yet to hear any account, however tentative, of what things look like to someone on the far side of this particular hurdle may give to some of the hesitant the confidence they need to take their own next steps.

Here, then, for what it is worth, is a brief description of where I find myself. Beginning from the question, 'How does our christian faith bear upon contemporary events?', I discover first of all that I can no

16

longer give the answer, 'Through direct manipulation by God in response to requests'. John Kent has put the matter succinctly.

'If I get news of the illness of my aunt, I may ask God to make her well again. The picture suggested is that at my request God puts in a finger and sets right what had been going wrong. The notion was perfectly credible in earlier years, but not now. When men believed in fairies, or when the RAF believed in gremlins, it was possible also to believe in the finger of God: today the whole category of the supernatural has faded out. This kind of simple intercession is not the whole of prayer, but it is significant: when it is discredited, the rest is discredited with it' (4).

If the old answer will no longer do, is there another? I can best express what I have come to believe by saying that it is in the ground we have been given for our hopes that our christian faith bears upon contemporary events. In this case christian prayer is the reminding of ourselves and one another of the facts about Jesus, and exploring together the implications of the facts about Jesus in order that on the basis of those facts and implications we may build our contemporary hopes, make our contemporary choices, and formulate our contemporary policies and plans of action.

The objection which springs to the lips of traditionalists at this point is that to describe prayer in this way is to reduce it to a mere thinking before one acts, and to rob it of its distinctiveness. Anyone, after all, can reflect before doing: that is not christian prayer but common prudence. Common prudence, however, has not necessarily anything to do with hope. What distinguishes prayer from prudence is the hope on which reflection is based. And what distinguishes christian prayer is that the ground of our hope is Christ.

This hope goes further than expectation based on observation. In fact, it often runs counter to such expectation, for the hope is based on a belief about the way things are, whatever the appearances. It is a belief that in and through history something is being established – a sovereignty, a kingdom. Prayer is action undertaken in that hope, because of that hope, in pursuit of that hope, in exploration of that hope.

This is the point which John Kent is working towards, but which I feel he does not quite reach, as he considers his fictitious aunt and her illness.

17

'Paul van Buren has suggested that when we believed in miracle rather than medicine, prayer was the appropriate response to the news of her need, but today the appropriate response is to take action: following that thought I might immediately rush round to auntie's house with a bunch of grapes. However, if I take time to reflect, I might consider that auntie is well off and probably has grapes and medicine well organised. It might occur to me that auntie could do with cheering up, so I could just go for a chat. Further reflection might suggest that she is old and frightened, and the biggest help to her might be to have someone to share her fear. Or she might be just tired and not wany anyone. My final conclusion is that I ought to visit her, take her a book she might enjoy, and be ready to talk about anything or nothing. In the end, I have responded to the news neither with superstitious knee drill nor with blind action: I respond first with taking thought'. (5)

But there is something prior to that. It is the belief that auntie is worth bothering about at all anyway. More, the amount of painstaking thought and action he is prepared to devote to her will depend on how much worth bothering about he believes her to be. It is in answering the question 'How much?', or 'How many times shall my brother sin against me and I forgive him?', that he shows himself a Christian or otherwise.

For the Christian, the dimensions of the hope on which his reflection and action are based are to be found, above all, in the record concerning Jesus. That is why, whatever else we may bring in to awaken us to the word that God is speaking to us, christian worship will always be centred on the Bible. There, in the record concerning Jesus, we believe we see what human life is all about, what kind of kingdom is struggling to be born. There too we see how different are the actions based on that hope from those based upon ordinary human expectation. 'Only power works,' says human expectation: but Jesus replies, 'Let him who would be greatest become servant of all,' and does so himself. 'All human endeavour comes to nothing in death,' says human expectation: but Jesus replies, 'Be steadfast, immovable, always abounding in the work of the Lord, forasmuch as in the Lord your labour cannot be lost.' 'Suffering is always hateful and unproductive,' says human expectation: but Jesus replies, 'Suffering willingly undertaken for the sake of others is heavenly and redemptive,' and again suits deeds to his words.

And so one could go on. Christian prayer is human reflection and action based on christian hope. And christian hope is what results from the belief that things are as Jesus declares them to be, rather than as they usually appear to be. Suppose, to add another example to that of Mr. Kent's aunt, that news comes to us of an area in which there is famine due to drought. What is best for us to do to help? According to an older view of prayer we should devote ourselves fervently and earnestly to asking God to send rain. Today we might feel that such prayer is not the kind we can confidently make, and should want instead to finance the digging of wells. But why should we want to do that for those people? Are they worth the diverting of money, energy and skill from other purposes and projects? On some grounds the answer might well be 'No': but reflection which is grounded on Christ would have to answer 'Yes'.

Prayer described in this way is, then, as much 'through Jesus Christ' as prayer described, in the traditional way, as request which can only 'reach' God and invoke his action if it accords with the mind of Christ. Here are a life and a death which happened, and to which, once I know about them, I stand in a relation either of indifference or of response. If my response is positive, and I find in the life and death of Jesus reason to believe that human life and love are more meaningful and more enduring than I had dared to suppose, I find myself with a quite new focus for my efforts and quite new criteria for my judgments about what to do and what to attempt.

But it is not easy to know what decisions to take in detail. I need to confer with others who share my basic point of reference. I need their help in getting the point of reference right, and together we need one another's help in deciding where we go from there. Perhaps this means that we may expect to find in the worship of tomorrow that our prayers, though still 'coming from God and going to God' in that they stem from, and help to realise, the hope he has given us in Jesus, are more and more addressed to one another. But now I am using 'one another' to mean not only our fellow members of the christian fellowship, but all those to whom our thankfulness is due, our penitence, our service in Christ's name. Indeed it is vital that the meeting of Christians in a local congregation does not become the self-indulgence of an inward-looking mutual admiration society — or even mutual castigation society. The trust and respect in which we hold our christian fellows, and which impel us to seek their forgiveness, their advice, and their acceptance of ourselves and our gratitude, must always stand for, and always lead out into, our relationships with others, both those

19

whom we do meet in the ordinary occasions of daily life, and those whom we shall never meet but with whom we are nevertheless bound in the bundle of life and for whom we can never disclaim responsibility.

This is the other great area of encounter with Christ which must come to find more and more representation in the worship of tomorrow. If the first is 'Christ in mouth of friend', this is 'Christ in mouth of stranger'. Just as I believe that occasions of worship need to contain more occasions of actual meeting between worshippers, whether in discussion-groups, in the momentary buzz of conversation, in a break for coffee in the middle of the service, or simply in the formalised greeting of the 'Peace', so also I believe that we must be feeling our way towards designs for corporate worship which do not involve our turning our backs, however temporarily, on those who need our help, and whose only way to find the gracious God may be through the discovery of a gracious neighbour.

It seems likely that such designs will involve more use of the newspaper, particularly perhaps the local newspaper, not only in the preparation of worship-material but in the course of the gathering itself. Our learning Christ from one another's faces may well take place as we talk together about how best to serve others whose condition we have been hearing about together.

The point about redirecting the address of our prayers from 'God' (meaning God-out-there, transcendent, third-party) to 'man' (meaning God-in-here, immanent in me and my neighbour and between us, first-party or second-party) was brought home to me vividly by a page in our missionary magazine. Beneath four striking photographs of people in different walks of life, and of different race, appeared this caption:

'These all look to you to give them their food in due season.
When you open your hand they are filled with good things;
When you hide your face they are dismayed;
When you send forth your Spirit they are created.'

I read right though to the last line thinking that the 'you' meant me. Only when I reached the sending forth of the Spirit did I realise that the whole caption was a quotation from Psalm 104, where the 'you' is God. Yet I still could not feel sure that my first thought had been wrong. I could hear Jesus saying to the disciples, 'You give them something to eat,' and then, on another occasion, when they asked him whether some words of his applied to them, saying, 'Who then is the faithful and wise steward, whom his master puts in charge of all his household to give them their food in due season?'

It *is* to us, their fellow humans, that hungry men look, and are meant to look, for food. When they pray, 'Give us today our daily bread,' they address the Father not by turning away from us, the brothers, but by turning towards us and saying it to us in God's name. When I open *my* hand, those who else would be hungry are filled. If I hide my face they are dismayed. Psalm 104 needs to be read alongside Isaiah 58. 'Is not this the fast that I choose ... to share your bread with the hungry, and bring the homeless poor into your house; when you see the naked, to cover him, and not to hide yourself from your own flesh (i.e., at the very least, your fellow clansman, and at best your fellow human being of whatever tribe or race)?' And when we manifest in our reflection and send forth in our actions the Spirit which is not our own but which has been given to us, the Spirit of Jesus, then those who are touched by the actions 'are created'. To all intents dead, they are brought to life again, made anew.

I am still not sure which way I was meant to take the caption. If the ambiguity was deliberate, it was more than just a clever idea. It is profoundly true that man must look to his neighbour for grace; but also that he will not find it in him except to the extent to which his neighbour has the spirit of Jesus. It is also true that if he finds grace there he will be moved to fall down and worship his neighbour: and that the neighbour, even if he be Jesus of Nazareth himself, must always deflect this right and proper worship-reaction towards the source of all goodness and all grace. 'Why do you call me good?' (Mark 10:18) 'Am I in the place of God?' (Genesis 50:19) 'Do not worship me! I am a fellow servant with you ... Worship God' (Revelation 19:10; 22:9).

Say, then, that the church is like the innkeeper in the parable, charged with looking after, out of its own resources for the time being, the wounded traveller whom the Samaritan has introduced to it. In that case the crisis in ministry will resolve itself into questions of 'how?' How much of its own resources should the church spend on the traveller? All, in one tremendous gesture *à la* Colin Morris, purchasing credibility at the price of oblivion? (For we need not expect, if we make such a daring and dramatic leap of faith, that any legions of angels will come and bear us up lest we dash ourselves to pieces on the economic rocks.) If not all, what proportion? And what sort of inn should it be trying to build with the rest?

The answers may well be different in different situations. In the city, where anonymity may be meat to some but is poison to others, the church must be structured in such a way that it can offer a welcome, a place where a person can know and be known, a context in which he may seek and keep his own identity. Yet at the same time the church must be sufficiently sure of itself not to devour him, as cannibals devour their victims, for the sake of assimilating his strength to itself. If he wants to, he must be allowed to go away and get lost at any moment. Such a city fellowship must be extremely alert and sensitive and unworried about its own future if it is consistently to gauge correctly the moments when someone needs rescuing and the moments when he or she needs to be left alone.

The trouble is that alertness and sensitivity are more likely to be found in small groups, while freedom from worry about its own future is more likely to be found in a large group. Maybe the pattern for the future in an urban parish is a number of small groups, affiliated to (or federated into) a larger group, the constant concern of which will be to make sure, by rearrangement as well as by verbal reminder, that the smaller groups remain genuinely open and accepting, and do not turn in on themselves.

It will not particularly matter whether these groups are found within present denominational boundaries or across them. Denomination is largely irrelevant to the task of being the church in the world of tomorrow; unless perhaps it can be shown that some types of organisation are more conducive to the required openness than others.

Having said that, I am aware that the individualised terms in which I have stated the church's task, the 'soul-by-soul-and-silently' approach to the innkeeper's role, do themselves betray my limited and denominationally-conditioned outlook. Must not the christian presence be so structured that it can stand in relationship to the local community as a whole as well as to individuals within it? Here I confess that the 'gathered church' principle, the voluntary association of Christians to worship and work together, has little to offer, especially in the large metropolitan areas where travel is easy and people often neither live nor work in the neighbourhood of their church. As far as I can see, the same voluntary principle, aided and abetted by high population density and the consequent proximity of parish churches to one another, has unfitted the anglican church, also, for any realistic neighbourhood-identification. It seems quite possible that the breakthrough here will come from the development of neighbourhood schemes of social service, engaged in by the Christians of that

22

neighbourhood, irrespective of denominational background and affiliation.

Only the Christians? In the realm of social service, Christians could do far more in the way of making common cause with others who share their social concern. But what then of worship? Any group of people who are doing a job together, in which they have their hearts, will find before long that they need some ritual celebration and summarisation of their common commitment. The obvious starting-point is still a meal. And if those of differing religions or none bring to that meal their own interpretations of its significance, what matter? Can they not share them with one another?

The foundation of worship, (and afterwards its further product) is a realised and self-aware community of commitment. This is something which has historically been stressed by Congregationalists in their practice of drawing up church covenants. The covenant, agreed on by all the members, expressed, sometimes briefly and sometimes at great length, the common basis of faith and intention of the local fellowship. Once a year, or more often, it would be read out, in the context of worship, as a sort of explanation to the world of why those people were there and what they thought they were doing.

It has become as difficult now to draw up a covenant for a Congregational church as to draw up a plan of instruction for church membership; more difficult, if anything, since the pictures thrown up by modern theology (e.g., 'the journey inwards', by John Robinson out of Dag Hammarskjöld) often seem more suited to individual meditation and mystical aspiration than to corporate acts. It is true that people taking psychedelic trips should do so in company. But this is not because they can travel together; rather, it is so that one may hold another's hand for reassurance as he makes his utterly private journey.

Once a group has come into being for common action, and has begun to grope towards ways of expressing and celebrating its community (not to mention advertising its whereabouts to anyone who may be looking for it), the question arises of its relation to other groups with the same or similar aims and of the celebration of this wider community. Part of our trouble and confusion about worship and church buildings and so on today is that we do not take enough notice of the difference between group-celebrations and crowd-celebrations. Crowd-celebrations (a football match is the obvious example) are characterised by vociferous excitement, release of energy – by spectators as well as players – and vicarious participation in a ritual

23

struggle. For any one person present, all that matters about the others is that they are there too. Whether he knows them, trusts them, likes them, has anything else whatever in common with them, is totally irrelevant. Group-celebrations (take a wedding reception or a funeral gathering) are like the other only in that they are special occasions and that they have a focus 'out there' — on the field in the one case, in the grave or the equally untouchable integrity of new marriage in the other — where we cannot go ourselves.

The contrasts are far greater than the similarities. Group-celebrations are (relatively) quiet, exploratory; people are reaching out towards one another; they are involved not vicariously but directly; their like or dislike for one another, intimacy or strangeness, are all-important. The ritual is not that of struggle, but of support and solidarity, suppression rather than expression. If conflict appears, the object of those present is not to egg it on to a decisive conclusion, but to minimise it, settle it, enwrap it safely within the multiple filaments of the group nexus, and put it in its place.

Between them these two very different kinds of corporate celebration account for a great many Saturdays for a great many people. Yet no one ever mistakes one kind for the other — no participant, anyway — though an observer might meet a group returning from one or the other and be unable to tell, except by its clothes, which it had been to. In either case he would expect it to be happy, fulfilled, lit up.

Participants in worship, as dwindling Free Church congregations know it today, have nothing like the same certainty about which kind of activity they are involved in. Most services have some of the aspects of one and some of the other. Sometimes the confusion is wilful: I know a congregation of fifty or so, certainly not a crowd, where the organist often plays at a volume and pace appropriate only in an Albert Hall crowded to the roof. Such delusions of grandeur apart, there is a genuine and general failure to distinguish between the two sorts of occasion which has many unhappy and confusing results. In catholic countries the church's feasts are clearly crowd-occasions, not unlike football matches (ritual struggle and all). At the other end of the scale, much revivalist worship is essentially of the crowd-type too. The Free Churches have tried to enshrine some of the solemnity and excitement of crowd-occasions: but nothing can really disguise the fact, once the distinction has been seen, that free church worship belongs to the group-style rather than the crowd-style. The participants depend on

24

one another as visitors to the Mass do not. Whereas in crowd-type churches it is buildings that have atmosphere, with us it is congregations that have atmosphere. They help one another listen or not listen, grow or not grow. Their meeting before and after worship is the meeting of people who know one another, are people to one another, liked or disliked: and it affords something for their lit-upness to perch on and feed on.

Yet it is possible to value this group-type gathering and still to enjoy occasional excursions to crowd-type worship. People come back to their local churches from assemblies and testify that they found them inspiring. The trouble starts when they begin to wish they had the best of both worlds at once, see that they have only one, and become depressed or anxious because they have not the other. Our excessive worry about declining numbers stems (where it is not purely economic) from the fear that you cannot have proper worship unless you have a crowd in each place. The truth is, rather, that it is enough to have a group in each place, and that from time to time groups should arrange to coalesce on a big enough scale to make a real crowd instead of a pretence at one.

It is in group-style gatherings that Christianity can make itself most accessible and useful to the people of the city. In the crowd they can only lose themselves as people: but they must first be enabled to find themselves. The organisation and training of manpower should accordingly be concentrated on the fostering of groups. Obvious social and personal needs are manifold enough to give plenty of focus for as many as a neighbourhood will hold. There is nothing whatever to be gained by doing such organisation and training denominationally once the denominations have seen and agreed on the object of the exercise. And by far the greatest part of the leadership work in the church so organised could and should be done part-time, by people who have a real stake in the community where they are, and who belong to their group (or group of groups) from within, instead of, as at present, arriving from what appears to be another plane of existence, fostering the group from outside and above, and then going home to their ministerial cloud.

It is a question, of course, to what extent anyone is immobile enough in today's urban situation to have a stake in the community where he happens to be at any given moment. Nevertheless there are communities other than the residential − professional and vocational groupings, clubs for leisure activities, and so on. Most Christians in the city have a stake in more than one.

Will there be any place in the coming church for the full-time professional? In terms of practical politics, he will probably see to it that his place is kept for him longer than it ought to be or needs to be. But it is extremely doubtful whether we ought to be accepting any further candidates for 'the ministry' conceived of as normally full-time. The latest regulations about training for the Congregational ministry, redrafted in 1970, state, 'A candidate shall be expected to offer himself for full-time service in the Ministry'. (Note the tell-tale capital.) This provision, which appears in writing for the first time now, means in effect that a man or a woman will not be accepted for theological training and commissioned service among our churches unless ready and able to cast his or her vocation in the mould of being 'a minister' in charge of 'a local church'. My guess is that the numbers of those so willing and able will dwindle almost to nothing during the next few years (they are already down to a trickle); while the numbers of those willing to undergo training in order to make themselves theologically literate and then work in, and round the edges of, local and professional and occupational church groups on a voluntary and part-time basis will increase.

Some will still be needed full-time. There must still be a strategy for the christian presence in a population, as well as tactics. Some administration, some fund-raising, some direction of training and research. Some specialists, moreover, to staff and organise the crowd-style moments. (They will want watching very carefully; but it would be silly to deny that some have the particular gifts needed for this necessary task. They should do it.)

But although for myself I have never regretted either the decision to offer to be a full-time minister, or the kind of training I received in order to become one, I think that if I were starting now, at this end of all the changes which have come to the church in the twenty years of my ministerial service, I should certainly wish to obtain a non-ministerial qualification, not only so as to be more than a virtually unemployable journalist if my ministerial role were to fold up under me but also so as to be able to take my full place, as an equal with those who are now my 'flock', in the life and work of the new pluralist society which is coming to be, in which human beings are permitted to be free, mature and responsible, and which, to my mind, is recognisably the fruit of the christian gospel. And when the committee asked me, 'Do you offer yourself for full-time service in the Ministry?' I should
26

now have to reply, 'Because I am not a scholar, or administrator, or crowd-person, I cannot say so. And I doubt if the day after tomorrow I shall even know, except in memory, what you mean.'

Notes

1. By John Stoughton, D.D. (London 1883). Dr Stoughton had been the congregation's minister for thirty-two years (1843-1875) which included its removal to its present site.
2. In conversation at the editorial board of 'New Christian'.
3. In an unpublished paper given to London Congregational ministers in January, 1970.
4. 'While walking the dog', 'New Christian' no.115, February 1970. p.9.
5. Ibid.

SERVANT OF THE SERVANTS OF GOD
by Neville Clark

It was a conference of clergy, doctors, psychiatrists, social workers, intent on exploring the problems of religion and mental health. One of the lay speakers caustically remarked that most church fellowships could hardly be viewed as potential centres of mental health – and he added, for good measure, that the ministry as a group was open to heavy suspicion at this point. Predictably enough the hall rippled with the nervous uneasy laughter of progressively-minded clerics. And the only non-christian psychoanalyst present murmured to me, with bewildered seriousness, 'Why are these Christians so uncertain and insecure?'

Certainly, at the heart of the church, there is an inner insecurity that is sapping its life. Of recent years we have lived in the midst of an orgy of self-criticism and a frenzy of self-reproach that has about it the smell of death. I am not referring to sober self-examination, constructive dissatisfaction, or healthy striving for reformation or revolution; nor am I defending complacency. I am speaking of a disease that afflicts the church, a compulsion to self-destruction, which betrays itself in the significant fact that some Christians actually seem happiest when they are verbally turning upon the church to rend it. This is not a fad of the time. It is a sign that the very foundations are crumbling, that a crisis of faith is upon us.

At the heart of that crisis stands the ministry. Inevitably it is there that the crisis is most keenly felt; for the ministry is, as always, the sensitive barometer that registers the shifting pressures. To probe the ministerial function and frustration is to expose the problem and possibility of the church itself. Such an enquiry cannot but be prosecuted from a limited perspective. That it is here attempted by one who has spent the last decade of his ministry in a suburban church that is still sheltered from the worst of the storms that rage is a factor that the discerning will want to take fully into account.

For the minister, particularly the younger minister, this is an era of self-questioning. No longer can he exercise his ministry unreflectingly and unselfconsciously. He stands back and looks at himself. He asks what he is doing, and why, and to what end. Sometimes he cannot answer his own questions. When he can, he is often horrified by the conclusions. The elements and factors contributing to his perplexity or his frustration are diverse and many. Some of the most important must be distinguished.

The contemporary minister is deafened by conflicting voices, claims, and expectations. There is the ecclesiastical claim, the expectation with which the church community confronts him. He is to represent the past in a world that is spinning crazily from change to change. He is to service the familiar structures, tune the motors, oil the wheels. He is to ensure constant numerical and financial increase, or at worst to hold the line and halt retreat.

There is the secular claim, the expectation with which the world in which he is set confronts him. He is to be a man of the modern scene, abreast of its fashions and attuned to its newness. He is to put himself at the service of human need and be foremost in charitable enterprises. He is to sanctify every civic good work, by his presence or by his blessing. He is to play the inspired amateur in every direction of the compass. At all costs he is to be relevant.

There is the personal claim, the expectation with which he confronts himself. He is to be the hero of faith, the knight of God. He is to sense the *kairos* and be obedient to its urgent summons. He is to track down his Lord and share his cross with him. He is to locate the crucial points of the advance of the kingdom, the decisive areas of the divine engagement, and take up his station there, booted and spurred. He must count, be significant, make a difference.

Diverse claims! Different expectations! The descriptions of them may be faulty, but the question of accuracy here is not of primary importance. Indeed, to identify the exact nature of the various claims will not necessarily take us very far. What counts is how the minister hears the claims; and his hearing is likely to be distorted by all kinds of presuppositions and assumptions.

In any event, the overwhelming likelihood is that the expectations will conflict. They war against each other. They pull in different directions. Is the church to write the agenda? Or is the world? Or is God? To frame the question in such a way might seem to lead inevitably to the third option, as being the unimpeachable and orthodox conclusion. Yet the difficulty is that the option is illusory. It is only another way of stating the question. Agendas do not drop from heaven. How does the divine secretariat communicate? Through the ecclesiastical post? Or via the secular communications system? The conflict of expectations remains.

The contemporary minister is also and therefore deeply conscious of inadequacy and lack of success. He is a divided man who finds

29

himself incapable of properly fulfilling any of the expectations that confront him. He satisfies neither church, nor world, nor himself, and that being so he sees little reason for believing that he satisfies God. He fits uneasily into all the roles that are pressed upon him or that he presses on himself, partly because his training scarcely seems to have equipped him for any of them. He is the eternal amateur, and as such inadequate. Try as he will, his efforts seem to produce little tangible result.

The contemporary minister is, in this situation, deprived of former supports and status. This is true at levels both superficial and profound. The payment offered him is by conventional standards derisory. The community at large no longer accords to him high status. Increasingly he lacks an accepted and significant place in society. The doubts and confusion he feels about himself are neither allayed nor counterbalanced by the verdict of others. Rather are his perplexity and insecurity confirmed.

At the same time he finds himself the representative of a shrinking institution. He serves a community which is visibly in decline and which seems increasingly to be relegated to the circumference of life. His predecessors might have been able to convince themselves that they were dealing merely with a temporary recession, and that, given patience and endurance, the tide would speedily turn. But he has lived through the full cycle of calls to repentance, evangelism, mission, and renewal; he has studied the signs of the times; and in his heart of hearts he knows that, humanly speaking, revival is not just around the corner.

Yet the problems go deeper. For in this predicament the minister often finds himself no longer undergirded by a deep community of faith. Moderators and Superintendents notwithstanding, this is not primarily a question of the need for a 'Father in God' or *pastor pastorum*. It never has been. It is rather a matter of the health of the people of God. For when the life of the church is deep and true it is the congregation that acts as corporate 'Father in God' to the minister. Nothing more pointedly underlines the present malaise than the widespread vacuum here. The result is crippling. It is the minister who must be unceasingly injecting faith, courage and expectancy into the community. There is little two-way traffic. So the strain upon one man's spiritual resources is tremendous, and sometimes becomes overwhelming.

Nor is this all. The minister similarly finds himself no longer undergirded by an atmosphere of belief. Today the whole fabric of
30

Christianity is under attack. Once, the basic realities of the christian tradition seemed to be unchallenged and impregnable, however violent the controversies or however pervasive the indifference. Now, the foundations are shaking. The minister finds himself no longer operating from a generally accepted base. He works against the backcloth of a crisis of belief, and whatever may be the extent of his own faith and faithfulness he cannot remain entirely insulated. Whether he likes it or not he is a man of his time. Whether he realises it or not his confidence and conviction are sapped or steadied by cultural assumptions.

Deprived of traditional supports, deafened - by conflicting expectations, and deeply conscious of inadequacy and failure, the contemporary minister may become, not surprisingly, a guilty and frustrated man. In so far as this is so, he must come to terms with himself, one way or another, or else succumb. The more intolerable the situation, the more drastic is likely to be the response made to it. Guilt and frustration which cannot be borne may be projected outwards and unloaded upon the church. The unsolved problem is exported. Relief is purchased by arraigning the church, its institutions or structures, its leaders or laity.

Not all can take this way, and since it subtly evades the heart of the problem such solution as it affords is likely to be partial and short-term. Many are led to the recognition that the confusion of role is the centre of the crisis, that it is this that is eroding their ministry. In the total contemporary situation the ministerial function must be clear-cut. So there is a tendency to seek role definition in various very specific directions. Two particular roads may be distinguished.

The one leads to some form of specialised ministry within the setting of the christian congregation. Perhaps the role of pastoral counsellor is appropriated. It has certain obvious attractions, and seems to provide the required liberation. It offers release from the cramping and archaic structures of the institutional church, providing a way of escape from that patient wrestling with committees and organisations for which their total lack of a theology of administration has left men ill-prepared. It offers release from the tensions of working within a group and with a mixed and resistant community, and thus assists the minister in functioning as the individualist his training is likely to have prompted him to be. It offers illusions of power, restoring self-esteem, and promising results. The other road leads to some form of specialised ministry on the frontier between church and world, perhaps in the field of industry, or of education, or of social service. Here also crucial

31

problems may seem to find resolution. The minister moves to the periphery of the organised church, and can feel that at last he can work unfettered by the confining limitations imposed by traditional structures, claims, and expectations. Status is restored to him. He has a man sized job to do, involving expertise, and gaining general recognition as significant and important. Most rewarding of all, he has recaptured relevance. He is serving at the growing points of contemporary life. He is where the action is.

To set a plea for the traditional ministry over against such exciting possibilities might be adjudged intolerable bathos. At least, if the venture is to be made, it must be done with proper awareness of the dangers. To opt for the familiar does not in itself settle any problems, nor does the decision carry with it any special immunities. The inherited ministerial role bears its own brand of temptation. It may provide a valued form of security. It may offer protection from the icy blasts of secular existence, a haven from the storm, a shelter from opposition, a shield against unbelief.

Subconscious motives need to be revealed. They do not however provide the material for all-embracing judgments. Specialised forms of ministry can present a theological and practical rationale, and in such terms they must be criticised, approved, condemned. The traditional understanding of ministry can and must do the same. A keen awareness of the distorting effect of personal need is the indispensable requisite for sound assessment. But it is in the light of other evidence and on the basis of other criteria that the final verdict is to be rendered.

THE ROLE OF THE CHURCH AND MINISTER

One thing seems certain. A clear definition of role is essential if the minister is to recover his sense of purpose. Yet no solution to this problem can be reached so long as it is considered in isolation. There is no direct route to an ultimately satisfying answer. For the confusion over ministerial role is intrinsically related to the current uncertainty about the proper role of the church itself. The prior theological questions concern the relationship of the church on the one hand to the world and on the other hand to the kingdom.

Adequately to chart that terrain would be an impossible task, given present limits. It may however be important to sketch in a few contours and delineate some significant options. There might be broad agreement with the thesis that neither church nor world can be equated with the kingdom. The kingdom in its fulness belongs to the *eschaton*.

32

In so far as it has come forward into history – and critically and centrally in Jesus Christ – it is operative in the world.

So far, perhaps, so good. What of the church? Suppose we say that the church is the vanguard of the kingdom, the bridgehead of the kingdom's victory, the representation of the kingdom in servant guise. What then is the function of the church? Just here the divide becomes more apparent, and no unanimous answer is likely to be returned. Is the function of the church to get lost, to become anonymous and in that sense to disappear, to locate the points where the kingdom is crucially engaged and to become there the hidden leaven, the kingdom's invisible weapon? In that event, the ministerial role would seem to be to pioneer the process.

This might be a justifiable programme for the *eschaton*. It is by no means clear that it is what is required of us 'between the times'. It is at least arguable that so long as – and only so long as – the distinction between kingdom and world remains, the distinction between church and world must visibly remain as well. It is at least interesting that the collapse of the church/world distinction is so often accompanied by the practical collapse of the kingdom/world distinction, with the consequent tendency to celebrate the secular in a curiously uncritical way.

It would seem to be truer to the theological realities to attempt a different definition. In the purpose of God the church is to be the visible representation of the new creation, the *pars pro toto*. That in turn dictates the ministerial role, by justifying the traditional understanding of that ministry as given for the growth to maturity of the Body of Christ. The ministry is the 'servicing' agency. The minister is the servant of the servants of God.

Such a ministry is clearly derivative. It does not constitute the church, nor does it stand in splendid isolation. The function of the church is to share responsively and obediently in the continuing ministry of its Head, proclaiming the gospel, being the reconciled community, participating in the ongoing redemptive mission of God. The function of the ministry is to equip the church to fulfil its obedience.

Against this background of understanding a clearer definition of the ministerial role becomes possible, and that in two directions. On the one hand it must be insisted that since the church is promised diversity of gifts it must recognise and elicit diversity of ministries. The minister is not normally or necessarily to be apostle or prophet, evangelist or

33

healer. He is to be faithful to his proper and distinctive commission.

On the other hand the minister must recognise in his own person a duality of role, in that he is the recipient of a double 'ordination'. Certainly he has been ordained to the ministry. Equally certainly and even more basically he has, by baptism, been ordained to the *laos,* the people of God. His life is lived within the tension and the possibility which this duality provides. As minister be embodies ministry to the church in a special and constitutive way. As layman he shares in the ministry of the church to the world. In so far as he is unfaithful to the demands of his baptismal calling, he distorts his ministry. In so far as he fails to distinguish the demands of his ministerial calling, he falls victim to crippling role confusion.

It will be sufficiently obvious that the point of arrival is what has traditionally been termed the ministry of Word and sacrament. On this understanding, the minister is the representative of the whole church of God to and in the local congregation. He is called and commissioned to exercise pastoral oversight in the bearing of Word and Sacrament so that the church may be conformed to Christ in ministry and mission to the world. Whatever may be the uncertainties about the form and structures of the church in the coming years, such a definition of the ministry can hardly be accused of necessary irrelevance. For whatever forms of churchly expression may prove to be the pattern of the future, manifestation in time and place is inherent in the church's visibility. Therefore, the church of tomorrow like the church of today will need to celebrate the supper and be set under the Word in order to grow to maturity.

Yet when all this has been said it may still be asked whether anything has really been solved. The classic reformed concept of the ministry is proposed; but is not the crisis, the frustration, the perplexity, to be found precisely in this ministry? Does this fact not expose the inadequacy of the traditional understanding, and conclusively demonstrate that it cannot and will not serve for the new day? The question is a fair one. It both demands and merits an answer.

The answer however cannot be a simple one, for the problems of the ministry do not exist in a vacuum. One important contributory factor is a widespread breakdown in congregational life. An effective ministry relates to viable churches, to communities which have the possibility of producing and nurturing a diversity of gift and of sustaining a proper mission to the places in which they are set. Conversely, no pattern of ministry will prove adequate for local churches that refuse to reform

34

and restructure their corporate life in obedience to the gospel and in response to contemporary needs.

A further significant element in the total situation is the crisis of belief in which church and ministry alike are involved. It is this reality that underlies the turmoil in which the ministry currently finds itself. The christian faith seems to be increasingly devoid of cash value in the marketplace. It does not always ring true or make sense in the minister's study. Yet it would be intolerably naive to imagine that a change in the pattern or understanding of the ministry would materially contribute to a solution. It might well prove to be an evasion of the full impact of the challenge.

What then remains? Probably two factors. One is the element of role confusion, which has deprived the ministry of chart and compass and which is partly the result of a failure to take the classic reformed definition of the ministry seriously. The other is the deepening sense that even the 'proper' work of the ministry fails to connect with the reality either of God or of man, that it has become a meaningless masquerade, that it has suffered an almost total evacuation of significance. Such a conclusion, whether it takes the form of a measured judgment or an agonised cry, cannot be lightly brushed aside. It prompts an honest reexamination of the ministerial task, even if, in the nature of the case, no more can initially be attempted than the raising of some basic questions and the framing of some guidelines for today and tomorrow.

At the centre of his calling the minister is turned in two directions. He serves the body of Christ. He serves the Word and sacrament. The one is defined by the other. His service to the body is nothing less and nothing other than service in Word and sacrament. So it is that his ministry receives form and definition from that in which he ministers. The secret, the wonder, and the scandal are brought to focus at his ordination. Into his hands he receives the Bible, the bread and the wine. Henceforth he is to bear and be borne by the Word and supper, for the health of the people of God.

It is therefore in liturgical assembly that the shaping of the ministerial task takes place. The Word is proclaimed. The eucharist is celebrated. Therein the ministerial role finds crucial and determinative expression. If there is a sense of irrelevance and unreality here, then everything else is likely to be affected. Crisis in ministry is subtly related to crisis in worship. That is why it is with proclamation and celebration that discussion must begin.

35

THE PROCLAMATION OF THE WORD

The proclamation of the Word of God to a christian congregation is not strictly and totally to be identified with the activity of preaching, at least not in the sense in which that has traditionally been understood. Such proclamation can take place outside the context of the church's regular worship. It is not essentially tied to the monological form.

Yet it remains true that he who would know the secret of proclamation must look to the liturgical assembly, and to that place where the Word determined by scripture thrusts forward towards its eucharistic enactment. Here the realities are unveiled. Here the theological lines and limits are revealed. Misunderstanding here will wreck proclamation wherever else and however else it takes place.

It is however just at this point that the ministerial problem is focussed. The sermon no longer communicates. It is doubtful whether it even has meaning. Over the years the preacher swings wildly and desperately back and forth between the biblical and the relevant. He must speak to the people where they are and as they are. So he assumes the prophetic stance, taking the individual problem, the national or international situation, and providing upon it authoritative comment and directive. To the secular situation he brings the christian answer. He starts where men and the world are. He finishes where men and the world ought to be. In between he seeks to preserve a space for the scriptural flavouring. He moves from the real to the ideal via religious sanctions.

But somewhere along the road the exercise turns sour. The preacher stands convicted of having sold scripture short. The christian gospel stubbornly refuses to be a detailed panacea for contemporary ills. The congregation obstinately refuses to move from the real to the ideal in living experience. The only relevance achieved turns out to be superficial. So the turn is made. Exposition becomes the central concern. The people must be instructed in the content of the Bible and the substance of the faith.

Now the movement is reversed. From the ideal to the real. From the text to the twentieth century, via the hallowed stages of background, meaning, and application. From the past to the present. From the answers to the questions. From the sacred to the secular.

Only somehow the journey is seldom satisfactorily made. The scriptural substance remains airborne and fails to touch down on contemporary events. Even if contact is established, a landing may seem impossible because the airfield is too narrow and confined. When a landing can be made, it is likely to prove almost too noiseless and successful. The intruder is deftly whisked to a convenient hangar and rendered inoperative. The airport continues its familiar bustling life, apparently supremely oblivious of the day of its visitation.

Gradually it dawns upon the preacher that communication has broken down at the most fundamental level. A yawning abyss separates the biblical from the modern world, and who can bridge it? The traditional christian concepts ring no revolutionary bells. The language of scripture is no longer the coinage of society. Speech about grace and guilt, judgment and redemption, either proves unintelligible or else evokes misunderstanding. The strangeness of the gospel is either domesticated, assimilated, distorted, or it is not heard at all.

Can preaching then, in any traditional sense, be still regarded as central? Must it not become a peripheral concern? Should it perhaps be discarded? Doubts born of despair seem to find justification from modern cultural and educational insights. Is not a revolution in communication, more basic than that occasioned by the invention of printing, upon us? Are not dialogue, discussion, participation, and activity the royal roads to knowledge?

To reject or to ignore genuine contemporary insights is obstinate folly. It is also a temptation to which those minds cast in traditional moulds are peculiarly open. Yet the issue is not to be resolved by a reference to Marshall McLuhan and a quick dismissal of the preacher as one who stands 'six feet above contradiction'. The tensions of the task must be lived with, not evaded. The urgent questions must continually be posed anew. What is the nature, and methodology, and vehicle of proclamation?

True and effective proclamation is the Word *becoming* Word. The minister stands, as representative of the universal church, within the ongoing tradition of the universal church, and offers himself and his words to the end that the Word there and then may become the Word here and now, in and to the local congregation. He comes with scripture in his hands; for the Bible within the body of Christ is the living Word of God, and no other means of access to that Word is open to him. He sets himself under scripture, that hearing he may speak, and·speaking may communicate.

And of course, in rush the problems. How is the transition from the there and then to the here and now to be effected? How is the Old

37

Testament to be related to the New? How is the meeting of two different worlds of thought to be effected? How transport the congregation to Mount Sinai, or shuttle the empty tomb into the modern sanctuary?

To wait upon the advent of a rounded and wholly satisfactory hermeneutical theory would be to wait for ever. Certainly the search must go on. But perhaps all that can be hoped for and all that is essentially required is a signpost that warns off false trails and indicates true directions. The preacher's task may be difficult. It is not impossible. It only becomes impossible when he totally misunderstands the nature of that Word with which he has to do.

The aim of proclamation is not to provide truth or knowledge, guidance or inspiration. It is to prepare the way for a confrontation between God and his people, the transforming irruption of God's future into our present. The preacher cannot evade his responsibility by claiming that only the working of the Holy Spirit can make his words the Word of God to and in the congregation, true though that be. Yet neither must he imagine that it is he who must impart to the Word of God relevance and life. He is the midwife assisting at birth, not the creator making dry bones live. The Bible does not have to be given life. It is the living Word. It does not have to be made relevant. It is relevant.

Old Testament and New Testament alike present one divine presence, one divine purpose, one divine speaking, and one divine acting, which have got themselves earthed in the actualities of human history, conveyed in the actualities of human speaking, and brought to burning focus in the actuality of Jesus the Christ. A story is told. It is an unfinished story; for it is not only narrative but also anticipation. With the completion of the canonical writing, God has not packed his bags and gone on indefinite vacation. That is why the task of the preacher is not the resurrection of a dead past by artistry and effort, nor is it to bludgeon a congregation back into the mists of antiquity to find God there. It is to re-enact the drama, to retell the story, in such wise that the depths of the contemporary situation are exposed and the hearers are brought to the startled recognition that they are 'on stage'. There is a chasm to be bridged and it is countless fathoms deep. But it is not a gulf between the Old Testament and the New, for as men 'in Adam', preacher and people alike live B.C. and as men baptised 'in Christ' preacher and people alike live A.D. Nor is it the gulf between the past and the present, the lengthening divide of historical time with all the cultural transformations that the years have brought — significant as this may be. Rather is the crucial chasm the one that gapes between the new world of God's redemption and the world of man's rejection, grown old, between the creative onrush of God's kingdom and the dying embers of man's proud striving. This is the great divide, the frightening gap, which the Word of God must bridge. And precisely herein, the biblical situation and every contemporary situation are at one.

So the lines are drawn and the nature of the task delineated. Yet the question of methodology remains to be faced. In what way is the preacher to understand the movement from scripture to sermon, and in what way is the transition to be effected? Let it be provisionally agreed that the text must be taken, that exegesis must take place, that the passage must be interpreted both in the narrower context to which it immediately belongs and in the broader context of the whole of scripture, that it must in some sense be understood in the light of Jesus Christ, that it must be related to the life of today. All this may be right and reasonable and necessary. It is not so clear that it will inevitably lead in the direction already chartered by the discussion of the nature of the Word of God.

Perhaps it is in the area of historical criticism that both the problems and the possibilities are most clearly unveiled. As the modern approach to the Bible gained increasing sway, the preacher was encouraged to take his historical consciousness seriously, and therefore to ask two crucial questions. With the scriptural passage before him he was to enquire, with relentless seriousness, 'what really happened' and 'what did it originally mean?'

Clearly the answering of such questions involved a probing behind the immediately given. It could no longer be assumed that things happened the way they were recorded. The facts did not lie on the surface. They were to be found at the end of a long chain of historical enquiry. They would emerge when the distorting layers of interpretation had been removed. Similarly it could no longer be assumed that the 'true' meaning coincided with that proffered by the biblical witnesses. A comparison of the synoptic gospels might seem to indicate that the evangelists had been more concerned to import alien interpretation than faithfully to reflect the mind of Jesus. The use of critical tools left many with the disturbing sense that the biblical writers showed an alarming and destructive tendency to obscure or misrepresent fact, to mask or manipulate meaning.

For an understanding of the methodology of the preaching task, the result was significant and in some cases disastrous. It was easy to conclude that the most authentic, valuable, and genuine material was that which was adjudged as 'earliest', in the sense of standing at least remove from the happenings to which it bore witness. In that event, it might seem likely that only an emasculated Bible remained for proclamation. The sermon rested on what was left when the onion had been critically peeled.

Nor was this all. Once historicity and authenticity were identified in this way, it was a small step to the implicit assumption that historical enquiry could, by establishing the 'facts', validate the biblical message. The appeal of the proclamation could become reasoned and reasonable, properly apologetic, safely secured. The sermon could lay bare the historical probabilities, build upon them, plot their inescapable corollaries, with the expectation that fair and open-minded men should accept and act upon them.

More important still, the use of the historical method pressed towards a pervasive sense of the 'pastness' of scripture. To use literary criticism was to underline that what was being dealt with was a book or collection of writings, an ancient library, a deposit from another age. To probe and probe behind the documents, seeking the actual event and the original interpretation, was to penetrate ever more deeply into the past and to accentuate the preoccupation with what once upon a time had happened or been spoken. The Word of God lay at the end of the historical trail, hidden in the there and then, and apparently confined by it.

So, in the initial movement from text to sermon, the preacher moved back from the present into the past, back from the world of today into the world of yesterday. Thereby he created the problem that thereafter dogged his steps. How return to the contemporary situation? How recross to the here and now? It was scarcely surprising that many retreated from the predicament, isolated critical knowledge from the preaching task, stayed firmly with the modern scene, sought scriptural answers to topical questions.

For those who could not take this way, however, the difficulty was acute, and a variety of unsatisfactory solutions was forthcoming. The particularity of the biblical witness could be overcome by detaching or deducing from it timeless ideals, truths or principles which could be painlessly shot across the centuries and deposited, shining with validity, on the shoulders of twentieth century man. Alternatively, the gulf of the years could be banished by treating the scriptural record as

40

exemplary, its characters as passable doubles of the people in the modern congregation, its predicaments as made-to-measure replicas of the contemporary churchman's situation, the divine verdict and command accordingly ready to hand, and the required human response patent and predictable — 'Go, and do thou likewise'! If, on the surface, the particularity of scripture was acknowledged, the salute was purely nominal and perfunctory.

The problems that literary criticism posed for proclamation are sufficiently obvious. What have not been so widely recognised are the possibilities which the further advance of historical method opened up, and the fruitful nature of the insights therein revealed. It is curious how little deep effect form criticism and redaction criticism seem to have had upon the preaching ministry. Certainly the necessity for and the importance of literary criticism remains. Yet it is in the context of traditio-historical enquiry that pressures emerge impelling towards an understanding of the task of proclamation more in accordance with the nature of the Word of God.

Behind the documents and their written sources lies the oral tradition. At once it becomes inescapably clear that scripture is not essentially a library to be read, and that to treat it as such is ultimately to take a dangerous and disappointing road. The Bible is first and foremost words spoken and heard, and therefore to be re-spoken and received anew. It is a story told, and therefore to be retold.

So behind the canonical record there must be prosecuted the enquiry into the history of the transmission of the tradition. To embark upon this task is to set scripture in motion, to set history on the march down and across the years. It is to dynamite all monolithic views of the unity of the Bible, to realise diversity in all its richness, and therefore to restore particularity to biblical understanding. For the picture that emerges is one of the constant reinterpretation of the tradition as in each new critical situation God travails with men. It is the picture of a contemporary 'word' ever and again being spoken which retains a massive identity with the 'word' that was spoken while yet possessing its own inalienable particularity. It is the picture of promise that is broken wide open by its eventual strange and unguessed fulfilment, and of fulfilment that betrays its incompleteness by generating fresh promise of that coming of God from the future which will make man's present new.

This does not mean that the preacher is suddenly released from the desperately searching questions that the use of historical method will always present. He must still ask himself 'what really happened?', knowing that no man's integrity must be sold short but knowing also that this is but the preliminary to proclamation. He must still ask 'what did it originally mean?', and ask it the more urgently since in the answering lies the check upon his own arbitrary dominance over the record. But beyond all this, his stance is now determined for him.

As he wrestles with scripture, he stands and must stand in the twentieth century. This is not to deny a proper and necessary immersion in the biblical world as the exegetical task is undertaken and discharged. It is to deny that the sermon itself can take shape from that perspective. In the setting of exegesis, the Old Testament must be dealt with from within the Old Testament world, the New Testament from within the New. But in the movement to proclamation, the Old Testament must be interpreted in the light of the New, and both must be heard and understood from a standing-ground in the present. This is the biblical writers' own stance. It must be that of the preacher.

For it is only within a contemporary setting that the Word of God can be heard. The sermon cannot allow the congregation to retreat into anybody's past. The preacher cannot allow himself to escape into scripture. If he takes that road he not only evades his responsibility but also renders the discharge of his task impossible. He ends up standing in the biblical arena, vainly trying to lassoo the twentieth century world. He has rendered communication impossible, by rooting himself in a place in which he cannot be addressed and from which he cannot speak.

He must then have the courage to come as modern man. He bears the results of his historical and exegetical enquiry, but he is laden also with the modern consciousness, his own self-understanding, his understanding of the world of his day. He confronts scripture from a vantage-point inalienably his own.

But he does not come seeking biblical answers to contemporary questions – and that for a more serious reason than the fact that the Bible does not provide such answers anyway. For the truth is that it is the Word of God that is waiting to set the terms of the questions themselves. Clearly this does not mean that the preacher moves towards proclamation as a contemporary man but with a blank mind and an empty heart. Rather is it that his posture must be one of listening, and his approach one of obedience. As he questions, he must be open to being questioned, and to find his provisional questions overturned and reframed.

If such is the kind of methodology proper to proclamation, it becomes clear why no neat hermeneutical theories are finally adequate and why no unvarying, detailed procedures can confidently be laid down. Warning lights may be erected. Directions may be plotted. But the circle cannot finally be closed. For when all that is required of him has been done, the preacher is brought at last to the place where everything has to be hazarded and nothing can be commanded.

Yet the Word of God can be communicated only through human words. Here also there must be conformity to the nature of proclamation. Any words will not do. Neither will slavish adherence to the words of scripture. There is a task of creative translation to be performed ever and anew. Communication can take place only as the Word of God becomes truly the contemporary Word, rooted in our modern culture, earthed in the twentieth century world of thought and life.

Just here the barriers are as high as perhaps they have ever been. The problem must neither be given false ultimacy nor be lightly underestimated. It must not be given false ultimacy, since the final and most serious obstacle to the hearing, understanding, and receiving of the Word of God is that it is a Word that comes in the teeth of human wishes and expectations, contradicting our desires and overturning our hopes. Yet it must not be lightly underestimated, since the assumptions of the age are so stubbornly resistant to those of the Bible. Nothing can now be presupposed − not even the reality of God. The christian assertions are not so much incredible as meaningless. Even in the ears of a christian congregation, the great biblical words sound like the echo of a forgotten language.

At this point, the pattern of scripture itself again becomes relevant. In the Old Testament, the Word of God comes to birth as the life of Israel interacts with constantly changing cultural situations. In the New Testament, that Word finds its rich diversity of enactment as the church comes to terms with the hellenistic milieu. In each case the struggle for communication involves a receiving and a transmuting, as current coinage is reminted and the linguistic highways of the contemporary world are bent and reshaped to carry strange traffic. The modern preacher falls heir to this continuing travail. The call is not for a superficial modernisation of traditional language but for something much more like a semantic shift. It is a terrifyingly difficult demand.

The preacher is not often in the best position to meet it. Perhaps the most disastrous gap in his training was a complete failure to confront him with the basic issue of the nature of language itself. He has to grapple with Heidegger and Wittgenstein, with Barfield and Merleau-Ponty. Is language merely a system of signs, readily detachable from thought which somehow lies behind it, arbitrarily attachable to an independent reality it somehow seeks to express? Is the truth of the gospel to be conveyed in language that denotes or language that connotes. If the Word and the words are inseparable, the significance of linguistic modes cannot be bypassed.

The situation is not made easier in so far as the preacher has been led to believe that the sermon is an instrument of teaching, and that it is rational explanation — albeit in simple terms — that the People of God require. The alert congregation expects that at the end of the day it should have learned something, that it should carry away truth perhaps not known before, which can be looked at and reflected upon at leisure. What seems to be required is conceptual clarity, persuasive logic, the arguing of a case, clearcut answers to perplexing questions.

Certainly the necessary element of rationality in the proclamation must not go by default. The Word has content. It does not bypass the mind of man. It has not reached its goal by virtue of the fact that feelings have been stirred and the emotional temperature brought to boiling point. Yet since it seeks encounter, it inevitably strives after a confrontation with the whole man. The aim of proclamation is to make room for a new world to supervene upon an old, and therefore to illumine common experience and to menace, claim, and engage the human will.

So it is that language cannot operate on the plane of flat scientific objectivity. It is inevitably to be shaped by the reality it bears. That reality promises solutions to no man's questions, but rather claims to light up every landscape and extend the boundary of every horizon. Words that are conformed to the Word of God must be broken, open, fluid words, tension-laden, evocative, poetry rather than prose. They do not argue a case or offer an explanation. They tell a story and expose a strange new world.

That is why the parables of Jesus remain paradigmatic for the preacher. For the parable is not concerned with making a point, illustrating a principle, imparting a specific directive or a fixed meaning, but with disclosing reality by ushering in the kingdom. It calls no man to to retreat into a sacred past to find and be found by God. It unfolds the ordinary world in its sometimes daunting, sometimes reassuring familiarity, and encourages its hearers to walk freely and attentively therein.

44

But then, suddenly and without warning the lightning strikes and the ground trembles. A new world is superimposed upon the old. The glass separating appearance and reality is shattered in pieces. The old order of man is gripped and fractured by the future of God. And men are caught, challenged, and forced to choose. So does the Word *become* Word.

THE CELEBRATION OF THE SACRAMENT

To define the ministerial role exclusively within the context of proclamation would be to expose it to disastrous misunderstanding. The minister is the servant of the people of God in Word and sacrament. He is called to proclaim. He is also called to celebrate. The interrelationship here is not accidental. It is necessary. It is in the totality of the liturgy that the shaping of the ministerial task in its fulness takes place.

For if from one point of view the movement of proclamation is from text to sermon, from another and equally important point of view the movement is from baptism to eucharist. The Word is spoken within the liturgy of the baptised. It is spoken to a christian congregation, to men and women who have already been given the freedom of the strange new world of God. It comes to those who have, in baptism, been set beyond the cross and resurrection.

Therefore it is the baptismal reality that gives the preacher his perspective. If he takes sin seriously, he takes grace even more seriously. Nor is this all. Origin is matched by goal, as the Word finds its terminus in eucharist. Faithful proclamation is bounded by remembrance and hope. It takes place when a congregation is set in motion, recapitulating the whole movement of christian initiation from baptism to supper.

For it is the celebration of the supper that provides the total context and the focal concentration which safeguard the proclamation of the Word against the perils of distortion. The thrust of the preaching has a specific and particular character, on any and every occasion. Partly this is due to the demands of a specific text and the situation of a particular congregation. Partly it is the result of the preacher's own limitations. Either way, there is the peril of a loss of balance and wholeness in the presentation of the gospel. It is the eucharist that surrounds the proclamation with the totality of the biblical story, in the rehearsal of the creative and redemptive activity of God. It is the eucharist that relates the proclamation to its one centre of meaning, in the showing forth of the death and resurrection of the Lord.

45

It is in the supper above all that the congregation is grasped and dealt with in its corporateness. If the Word is received by each man in his inalienable separateness, the supper is shared by all in inalienable solidarity. Here the containing walls of the isolated self are dismantled. Here a common participation in the one Lord is recreative of the one Body. Here a congregation, passing anew through the death and resurrection of Christ, is re-formed a christian community.

Yet it is just here, perhaps, that the ministerial problem threatens to re-emerge. The supper no longer proves meaningful in that it no longer impinges on reality. In the worst possible sense it seems to be a 'cultic' act — expressive of a false 'holiness'. It withdraws the congregation from the tensions of earthly existence, ministers to individual piety, and sucks men into otherworldliness.

So the urgent questions must be posed once more. In what way is the supper meaningful and relevant? How is it related to the world of man's striving? What is the true nature of celebration? One thing is certain. The sacrament cannot be invested with reality unless it first bears it. It cannot be filled with meaning unless it first carries meaning. It cannot be made relevant unless it *is* relevant.

So it is that discussion must begin with the realisation that the supper is the celebration of the world's redemption. It is the effective re-enactment of the reconciling travail of God with his creation, and therefore the unmasking of the cross and resurrection in the midst of life, time and history. To celebrate the supper is to set the congregation at the focal point of judgment and renewal, that thereby it may be hurled afresh into the ongoing mission of the Lord.

For precisely here the Body of Christ is led in the discharge of its priestly ministry. As it is grasped and broken and remade, it is not apart from the world it represents, but for that world and in unbreakable unity with it. It bears and leads mankind, exposing itself to the world and the world to God, hearing the cry of the hungry who lack bread, setting war and racism and injustice and sickness and the whole tangled muddle of human greatness and human failure beneath the shadow of the cross and at the entrance of the empty tomb and in the path of the arriving kingdom. This is common action, from which men may expect to emerge with something of agony and sweat still visible upon their brows. This is the unveiling of God's future within the very stuff of human existence. And as such it is the most profoundly secular act that, in this life, men are given to do.

THE ROLE OF THE PASTOR

It is only in the light of Word and supper, of proclamation and celebration, that the role of the minister in the exercise of pastoral oversight is rightly to be understood. His pastoral ministration is not some added responsibility, subject to different norms and directed towards different goals. It is nothing less and nothing other than the extension of his liturgical role into the totality of the life of the dispersed congregation. For the Word which moves to its inevitable sacramental concretion in the eucharistic drama of redemption presses relentlessly onwards towards actualisation in the corporate life of love and embodiment in the maturity of discipleship.

That is why the severance of pastoral oversight from its ultimate ground finally dooms it to irrelevancy. In his contact with congregational groupings the minister finds himself playing the part of private chaplain, honouring what happens to be going on with his expertise, hallowing it with prayer, and sanctifying it with his blessing. In his congregational visitation, he tacitly accepts the role of friend and brother, seeks to exude what warm humanity he can muster, and is welcomed as one who can be relied upon to show interest and concern. The divorce from proclamation and celebration is complete. Small wonder if at last the minister rebels.

What is the alternative? Perhaps the most obvious, and in some ways the most attractive, is to assume the role of pastoral counsellor. The minister, treading this road, can feel that his energies are realistically engaged at the places of urgent need, and that at last he is exercising a professional commitment to the task of healing. Yet the essential problem may well have been reframed rather than pressed through to a solution. For the danger is still that the norms which govern and the goals which beckon are grounded in and derived from something other than the fundamental ministerial calling.

The reason for this substantially lies in the nature of the counselling process itself, as it has been developed and understood in recent decades. The traditional pastoral approach, attitude, and practice seemed to contradict emerging psychological understanding, deny psychotherapeutic possibilities, and hinder growth to maturity. It was necessary for a drastic reorientation to be effected. The dynamics of personality were the foundation, case-work the method, healing the goal. The characteristic picture of counselling became that of the minister face to face with another individual, at the point of his weakness, confusion, and need, seeking to foster and establish the relationship and conditions within which insight could be born and healing effected.

A viable pastoral theology was almost entirely lacking. This alone should have been sufficient to set all the alarm bells ringing. Certainly the factors contributing to this situation were many. Yet among the most significant was surely the way in which the understanding of the counselling process failed to cohere with the basic and controlling realities of the ministerial calling.

This crucial incongruity is evident at three points. In the first place, counselling found paradigmatic expression in the confrontation of minister and 'client'. The framework was intensely individualistic. The implicit drive was in the direction of self-realisation. Yet because the minister finds his mandate not in the Word alone but in the indissolubility of Word and sacrament, his ministration has corporate rooting and must find corporate expression. Whether his pastoral task is being discharged in a group context or in the intimacy of a single personal encounter, he continues to deal with men in their interrelatedness. His model of pastoral care is not formed by reference to the counselling situation but is given to him in the liturgical assembly.

For it is the supper that irreversibly bars the gates against any attempt to minister to man in isolation from his fellows or in abstraction from the structures of the world which mould him. Here it is laid down that the redemption of any man is bound with the redemption of his fellows and the redemption of the created order. Therefore pastoral care must be inescapably communal in emphasis and must reach into the corporate and institutional rootings of human sickness and disorder. It means a pastoral theology which, in the light of the form and shape imparted to the congregation by and in the eucharist, must finally speak critically and creatively to the structures of society.

In the second place, counselling was inherently problem-centred. It specialised in the crisis situation. It was directed to men in the urgency of their weakness and need. Yet exactly at this point it served to confuse and limit ministerial understanding. For the pastoral ministry is not a breakdown service. It is directed towards the building up of the Body of Christ. Therefore it deals with men in their strength as well as in their weakness, in their normality as well as their abnormality. Indeed it is from this perspective and in this preparatory fashion that it makes its most significant contribution. It seeks to equip men that in the hour of crisis they may stand. It strives so to mobilise the forces of healing that when at last sickness strikes it may be overwhelmed. In ultimate terms, the goal of pastoral care is to prepare men in the prime of life for death.

Yet if the whole truth is to be stated, the argument must in some sense be reversed. In so far as counselling was problem-centred, it obscured the ministerial task by its tacit implication that sickness and need constituted occasional and special challenges. They were relatively exceptional excrescences in an otherwise tolerably healthy body. Yet the minister who finds his mandate in the Word must operate with a very different model of the human predicament. He has to reckon with the realities of sin, and therefore with a universality of need. The whole of his congregation shares with him a basic sickness, requires with him a continual healing. More truly still, the Word he is constrained to minister is a Word that strips away the superficialities of wholeness, and reveals and illumines the unconfessed and unsuspected weakness and alienation.

In the third place, counselling characteristically sought the establishment of the relationship and conditions within which insight could be born and healing take place. Guilt was to be alleviated, not confirmed and deepened by judgmental attitudes and reactions. Dependence was to be dispelled, not heightened by instruction and directive. Healing was the goal, interpersonal therapy the process, and acceptance the key. Yet here also the pattern fitted uneasily with the nature and imperatives of the ministerial calling. The minister, tied fast to Word and sacrament, is pressed inexorably towards proclamation and celebration. He is commissioned and impelled to bear the word and deed of God into the pastoral situation, and so to make room for the divine gift and presence that they may freely run their disturbing, renewing, and utterly relevant way.

This is not to deny the value of counselling in its own terms and within its necessary limits. Nor is it to ignore the changes in emphasis and assumption that have marked the last decade. Indeed it seems likely that, in its extreme form, non-directive client-centred counselling stands under sentence of death in the very land that gave it birth. Further and more positively, it must be insisted that pastoral ministration undertaken in disregard of contemporary insights into the dynamics of personality is likely to be limited and impaired, and that pastoral theology which does not come to birth through labour pangs

49

occasioned by the relentless pressures of modern psychological understanding is doomed to distortion. To evade the embrace of Hiltner or Lake is not necessarily to be driven into the constricting continental arms of Thurneysen.

What must be affirmed, however, is the fundamental inadequacy of the counselling model for the pastoral task. It is at once too limited and improperly conceived. To engage in pastoral care is to extend the Word and Sacrament into the life of the dispersed congregation. It is to celebrate the reconciliation of God amid the estrangement of men, to re-enact redemption in the fabric of relationships, to proclaim the word of judgment and renewal, to announce a kingdom that wills to be embodied in the stuff of living.

In the pastoral encounter, then, the concern of the minister is that men shall be laid open to God, gripped by his judgment, and surprised by his grace. There is a Word to be communicated which, because it is the Word of God, may search and sear and wound as it moves to recreate. There is a witness to be borne which contradicts what is, in the name of what may be and shall be. There is a cross to be implanted which reveals itself as the only gateway to renewal. For the minister deals with his people always and only on the ground of their baptism, seeking for and in both himself and them the constant recapitulation of the strange 'initiatory' road. He comes not to understand or to accept, but to attest liberation — though it will often be through understanding and acceptance that liberation is mediated.

Everything depends upon the establishment of a pastoral relationship which may become God's opportunity. In and with it all, the minister must learn to bear and to forbear. He will not speak too quickly, but will wait with unflagging alertness and invincible patience for God's moment. When he speaks his words will be broken, open words, born of struggle, welling up from a deep humanity, and pointing to realities that cannot be captured, domesticated, and owned. Since communication is more than speech, he must be master of many 'languages'. Sometimes his language will be silence, sometimes gesture, sometimes touch, sometimes simply his felt presence and participation. Yet since he is captive to the Word and supper, his pastoral ministration must ever be conformed thereto. He bears no bag of healing remedies. He carries no slick solutions to human need. He brings no answers to the questions of men.

He comes to celebrate the sacrifice accomplished and the victory won, that a life brought near to despair may look up and know that its

50

redemption draws nigh. He comes to spread the table of thanksgiving in a human heart, that a life embittered by the bruising pressure of the years may be caught up into the mysterious tides of grace. He comes to re-enact the cross and resurrection in the dark places, that a life disordered in relationships may be set towards communion. He comes to proclaim a Word of forgiveness, that a life ridden with guilt may recapture the freedom of the children of God. He comes to announce a Word that lights up common experience, that a life lived along the surface of the passing days may be disturbed with discontent and never be at peace again. He comes to attest a Word that bears God's future in all its judgment and promise, that a life imprisoned in its past may find the shackles broken and hear a new thing calling. He comes. So often he fails. Yet this is his commission. He has no other.

It is along such lines as these that the clarification of the ministerial role must proceed. To dispel role confusion is not, of course, to dispose of the crisis. It is however to set the ministry at the place where the crisis can be met with resolution and with courage. It is also to indicate the nature of the resources available.

Because the church is formed and re-formed by the Word and sacraments, those who are charged to proclaim and to celebrate will find an inalienable ministry today and tomorrow. The minister, in these terms, is essentially a representative man. He serves the congregation, yet he is not simply a congregational figure. Rather does he embody catholicity. For he is the gift of the whole church to the local congregation, set therein to promote its christological ordering and its growth in love, charged with focal responsibility for the integrity and relevance of its proclamation.

This does not mean that he is removed from the congregation in authoritative isolation, for his essential rooting is with them and among them in the totality of the liturgical assembly. Nor does it mean that he is removed from the world. Rather does obedience to his commission throw him headlong into the secularity of his time, directing him to the heart of the world's turmoil to receive the Word of God, and condemning him to be the battlefield where the conflict of faith with doubt is waged ever and anew. For he is a man bidden to stand on the frontiers of human existence, where God's future engages man's grandeur and misery.

Given such a role to play, the minister is provided with the materials for self-understanding. Here indeed a question is introduced that demands an answer. If the minister is to do his part faithfully, he requires to know who he is. The old familiar images – priest, pastor, shepherd – will not finally serve, partly because they lack meaningful rooting in the heart of the contemporary world. Against the background of the modern crisis of faith, as well as in the light of the essential nature of the gospel, new images must be found.

Perhaps it is Paul's self-portrait that provides the significant clue. 'We are the impostors who speak the truth, the unknown men whom all men know' (2.Cor.6:8-9. N.E.B.). Here the fundamental paradox and incongruity are starkly revealed. The minister is a man who bears and in some sense must embody the drama of redemption. He is in the public eye, yet he remains a nonentity, a 'nobody', an 'unknown'. He claims to speak the truth, but he is always open to betrayal as an impostor, for any man can rip off the mask and reveal him for what he is or seems to be. Thus is the offence of the gospel portrayed. For God comes to men only in human weakness, and God speaks to men only through faltering, human lips. And if this be true, then I suspect that the contemporary minister will find himself most truly identified in Berger's image of the 'clown'. For in the figure of the clown, the nonentity and the impostor are brought together. Here is a 'nobody' in the public eye. Here is an impostor, wearing a mask, who somehow communicates reality.

The ministry are God's court-jesters. In word and life and action they embody the crazy, incredible paradox of redemption, whispering the story to those who will listen, singing it to those who will rejoice, re-enacting it in the incongruity of worship. Their wild buffoonery overturns the familiar and the expected, and somehow opens a window into a looking-glass world, a kingdom unknown yet well-known, where only the childlike are at home. They tug at the heartstrings with a mad message that has taken possession of them and must constantly be relived and retold. They come as emissaries from another existence, proffering glimpses of a fantastic reality, which remain to haunt the human heart. They play out the strange part assigned to them, contradicting all the conventional assumptions and expectations, planting absurdity at the heart of the commonplace, lifting tragedy into the laughter of heaven, ushering on stage a strange, new, wondrous world. And they must continue to perform, even when their hearts are breaking. For they are the fools of God.

MINISTRY IN FERMENT
by Ernest Marvin

A QUESTION OF ROLE

I am convinced of two things:

(i) The role of the ordained minister is about to undergo trenchant change whatever his denomination.

(ii) There is a role for the ordained ministry.

But role-change, like the change of life itself, can be a trauma of such penetration that it leaves the parties involved with a severe problem of readjustment.

In the face of contemporary pressures on the ministry, two attitudes have polarised. At one extreme there are those whose strong inclination is to dig in their heels against the slightest suggestion of alteration in the transmitted function of the minister. On the other, there are many who are convinced that, if the mission of God is to be revealed at all in the midst of the contemporary world, then the necessary mutation which the ministry has to undergo simply cannot be fertilised within the septic structures which constitute the orthodox churches of today. Whichever end of the spectrum the minister belongs to, or even if he is placed firmly in the middle, 'ferment' is not too strong a word to describe the emotions of those involved. Of course, role-questioning is not confined to the ministry. It is a common-place amongst the professions: doctors do it, teachers do it, dustmen do it — everybody does it. Such questioning however, does not result in considerable numbers relinquishing their jobs. People do not doubt that there is a need for doctors, teachers and, especially, garbage disposal experts. But the poor parson is not sure if he is needed, never mind wanted, in the same way as his contemporaries are. He is resigning in increasing numbers, and 'poor' parson is right, for there is the little matter of economics.

Apart from employees of the Church of Scotland and anglican incumbents, most ministers in Britain are unlikely to be earning £1,000 a year. An american colleague, who recently worked as a member of our team in Bristol, pointed out wryly that the Presbyterian Church of England minimum stipend, which he was receiving for services rendered, was below the poverty level set by President Lyndon Johnson. Now the world certainly does not owe the church a living and it did not ask us to be ordained in the first place. But all the pious talk amongst Christians about vocations and stipends, as opposed to jobs

53

and salaries, ignores the fact that £1,000 today is not even a viable stipend. I have met some folk, usually in a higher income bracket, who do assume that it is adequate. I have even met some ministers who thought so too, though on the lamented demise of two of them, I discovered that they each had a private income.

As things are in Britain today, matters are going to get a good deal worse. Possible entry to the Common Market, the present escalating scale of wage demands, rising prices, declining membership and the inevitable decrease in church income, are already combining with a number of other factors to put the final skids beneath those who are holding on by the skin of their overdrafts and the wits of their wives. At the time of writing, the press has been carrying the story of twenty-four english clergymen engaged to participate in a TV commercial for the american market. They had been selected from an even larger group of clerical applicants. The product they were promoting was a razor blade. One of the conditions of selection was that they had to cultivate several days growth of beard. They finally appeared in the film, their stubbly chins sprouting over white collars like so many grinning gooseberries. Then, they shaved with the magic edge, and testified to its transcendent quality.

Perhaps the English were preferred to their american counterparts because they were more likely to wear a back-to-front collar and therefore the image would be established immediately. But undoubtedly another factor was that they were in greater need of the cash.

It has been the economic factor which has helped to tip the scales in many manses today when the inmates have decided, often painfully and reluctantly, that they have to get out. A good number of these ministers have other, deeper problems in relation to their role, but a more viable financial basis would have encouraged at least some of them to stay a little longer in the attempt to discover if necessary changes in their role could be achieved from within the present framework of the church. They see no point in working conscientiously on these issues if, at the same time, they are unable to support their families adequately. They have to be fools, perhaps, for Christ's sake, but not idiots.

However, even if all stipends were doubled tomorrow, and called salaries, painful problems would remain. After all, even to the most casual of glances it would appear that His Holiness Pope Paul is not exactly burdened by questions of personal finance. But he still has problems. We are not likely to see a wholesale defection of popes, or even cardinals, from the church in the immediate future — fascinating though such a prospect would be — but the fact is that, at all levels in the ordained ministry, from probationers to popes, there is a ferment at the heart of things and it smacks more of bewilderment than of vision.

AS THROUGH A GLASS DARKLY

It would be comparatively easy to demonstrate a variety of reasons for the modern parson's dilemma. Society today is highly urbanised and mobilised, whereas a minister's training is still more suitable for dealing with the parochial, if not rural, and static life of a previous generation. But to take each of these factors, and several more besides, and examine them individually, would be to give too much attention to the parts at the expense of the whole. For each relates directly to the overall cause of the present ferment in many a christian breast, and that is the movement of history which is called secularisation. It is this process which engenders bewilderment, fear, and suspicion.

It is a process which is far from being understood. From Bonhoeffer to Gregor Smith, and all stations in between, the tremors have reverberated throughout the church and beyond. But the practical lessons and applications resulting from what they have taught are only very slowly and painfully being learnt. Secularisation is a movement which is forcing many Christians to re-examine carefully what they mean by the world, the church and the kingdom of God, and what the relationship between them is. Popularly it has been associated with Bonhoeffer when he said that 'Man has come of age'. And unpopularly in recent years it has also been associated with the phrase 'The Death of God', coined by Messrs. Altizer, Hamilton and van Buren. Bonhoeffer did not live long enough to work out more fully what he meant, and the death of God theology has already committed suicide. But despite the over-use of the phrase 'Man come of age' and the transitoriness of the original views of Thomas Altizer and friends, secularisation is a movement which is speaking in a significant way to many Christians, and causing a serious appraisal of the church's mission and her structures.

Secularisation takes very seriously the doctrines of creation and incarnation. God made the world and it was good. And even when it 'fell' away from what he hoped it would be, he re-affirmed his faith in it by 'sending' his son to live as a man in the human situation. By his attentiveness to the world God has shown it to be the context within which he encounters man as a man, and where he expects man to

55

confront his neighbour and love him in turn. It is the only area where persons can meet and discover meaning and transcendence through the depth of their encounter. It must not be used as a training ground for part of a person which has been labelled 'soul', or as a stepping off point for heaven.

As it is the area within which God encounters man and loves him, it is also the place where he releases him and gives him his freedom. For if man is not free he is not able to respond in love to his neighbour and to his God. Nor, for that matter, can he be quite so loveable to his neighbour and to his God. Man, therefore, has to stand on his own feet if he is to be a man.

Now this is different from the pelagian and humanist notion of man pulling himself up by his boot-laces. His freedom is a gift, but it leaves him very exposed — laces undone, if you like. He is not helped to be any more of a man if God stoops to tie his laces for him. For if he is expected to do that where will it all end? Man will simply be dependent upon his Daddy and, in the process, will be less than a man, less than human.

And so God leaves man alone. Especially does he not try to usher him over into a small corner labelled 'religion' or 'the church', where perhaps there might be some protection from all the hazards of life which threaten to trip him up. Man need make no attempt to pull himself up, because God has already set him up. But he has to learn how necessary it is to tie his neighbour's laces and to allow his neighbour to tie his own in return. He has to learn to do this so that his progress can be smoother, so that there can be an encounter between people which is free of hesitancy and uncertainty, and which is spontaneous and natural and confident.

This expectancy has not been fully realised because of man's 'sin'. He has preferred simply to try to tie his own boot-laces or, if this is impossible, to keep himself on top by 'putting the boot in' on his neighbour. But then came Jesus: 'Behold the Man'. and the gift was there again for all to see, and to receive. Here was a man who was free for his neighbour and faced his neighbour at every point, even when it meant total rejection and his own death. Amidst this confrontation Jesus claimed in parable and in words that the kingdom of God was being revealed. The signs of its presence were the revelation of love in personal encounter and the making of life more human for others by encounter. And he called people to participate in revealing the presence of the kingdom by serving and loving. 'If I have washed your feet, so

56

ought you to wash each others feet.' Christ's goal was the revealing of the presence of the kingdom of God in the middle and the muddle of the human situation. It had always been present, ready to be discovered in meaningful personal encounter, but man through living to himself had lost sight of it.

Thus, the world is the area within which the kingdom has to be revealed in all its excitement. And insofar as the church is part of the world there ought to be signs of the kingdom even in the institutional life of the church, and especially in its liturgy. But this is only a part of the church's task, and perhaps the least important at present. Too much time has already been spent in the attempt to get people into the building, the assumption being that there something real can happen which cannot happen elsewhere. But the church is not the goal. The kingdom and its manifestation are.

The church is one of the agents in revealing the presence of the kingdom in the world, perhaps the chief agent. But God does not need any particular church, only the church which will serve and if she fails to do that he will look elsewhere for his agents of mission. It is much contention of some that this is precisely what is happening now.

The old missionary aim was that of bringing Christ to the heathen, and our missionary hymns still show how true this was. But to adopt such an aim was to forget that Christ was already there, present in the situation, and that the missionary's task was simply to reveal his presence. We hear the same assumption in some of our public prayers of approach to God. We say, 'O God, our Father, we come into your presence with thanksgiving', whereas a more accurate christian statement would be, 'We come into the consciousness of your presence.' And so, secularisation is forcing many Christians to re-examine their assumptions about the world, the church and the kingdom of God, and to work out the implications of their re-examination. It is precisely at this point that tension and bewilderment enter in.

This business of being free for the world seems to imply that we shall have less time to be free for the church. We shall not be quite so free to build up its membership, nurture its institutional life, care for its buildings, and plan its missions. And of course the secularist answer would be, 'Precisely! You ought to be spending less time on church affairs, and plan instead how, as Christians, we can participate more realistically in God's ever present mission to the world. How can we be the gracious neighbour? That is the question, rather than, 'How can we

57

get more people into church?'

I do believe there is a place for the worshipping community, and also that we cannot do without institutions and structures. But this conviction is still not adequate compensation for the problem posed to the ministry by secular theology. The minister is the paid servant of the church and therefore is more beholden to it than most. He may well see that the movement of secularisation is of the spirit and is to be welcomed. He may well agree that the church as an institution is not geared at all well to participate in this movement. But he also discovers that the necessary changes required are beyond his strength so long as he remains within the structure as a minister. His people, on the whole, do not know what he is talking about, and do not really want to know. For them the church is the goal, or the launching pad for heaven. The world provides too many hazards. It is best left alone, kingdom or no kingdom. Faced with the mammoth structural changes necessary if the church is to be able to reveal the excitement and the presence of the kingdom of God in the world, many a minister gives up.

'The problem of the contemporary structure of the church is that it was devised for a past form of society which was static, generally agrarian, and religiously conformist. Essentially the same structure was exported in the era of missionary expansion. It is, however, a fact that today this form of society is becoming increasingly a-typical, as urbanisation and industrialisation become characteristic of all societies. Underlying concomitants of this process are secularisation, pluralistic societies in which different value systems stand side by side, and a situation in which the church, unable to impinge in complex and dynamic forms of society, becomes insulated and cut off from the realities of social life. It is a dangerous temptation for the church to make a theological rationalisation of this situation, and to adjust itself to a peripheral role in society, thus betraying its essential mission.' (1)

Whether it is a 'dangerous temptation' or not, the fact remains that more and more ministers find today that they have either to accept an artificial and peripheral role, or else leave the ministry altogether. Amongst the latter there are many who would agree that 'the logic of the situation' does require a total re-structuring of the church, but for them commonsense also requires it to be recognised that this is impossible in the present state of the church. This is a view I can understand, but cannot altogether agree with and so I remain, for the

58

moment, an ordained minister of the church.

But I am in a polyglot company, many of whom speak a language which sighs for the old days and believe they might even return. But to sigh for the former things is to be blind to the reality which was the past.

THE EDIFICE COMPLEX

The church has been 'threatened' with the process of secularisation for a very long time now. Its origins go back as far as the collapse of·the medieval synthesis of church and state. The enlightenment of the eighteenth century accelerated the process. But the great missionary drive and religious fervour of the nineteenth century, combined with the outward success of the church at home in the west, succeeded in hiding the true situation from view.

In Britain the writing has been very much on the wall since the end of the second world war, although a faint scrawl was discernible before the first had even begun. So long as the mass of people seemed 'influenced' by religion the churches never doubted that they were in with a chance. And as in the nineteenth and part of the twentieth centuries, a man often could only obtain even an embryonic education if he was attached to either church or chapel, this influence seemed more real than it was.

It is astonishing to realise, as Kathleen Bliss reminds us, that as recently as 'the time of the 1944 Education Act nearly two-thirds of England's schools were church schools' and that,

'By 1800, about 600,000 children and adults were receiving religious instruction and learning to read and write in Sunday Schools. These activities and others like the class meetings of Methodism had to be housed, and thus began the new and most characteristic feature of nineteenth-century church-building, the complex of buildings containing halls, class-rooms, committee rooms, kitchens, common rooms, providing a space for a growing range of activities broadening out from the specifically religious to the more general social and educational, and providing for many age and interest groups. *Many more people used these buildings than regularly attended the worship of the church or chapel.*' (2)

It was natural that this kind of provision gave the church contacts with working class people which otherwise it might not have had. This contact was continued during the depressions of the twenties and early

thirties of this century in places as far apart as the villages of Durham, the valleys of Wales, and for that matter, the townships of West Virginia. And in those grim days in Britain the chapel also helped to provide political education for the rising member of parliament, trade-unionist, socialist and the like.

So while the hungry miners of Durham were throwing the establishment, in the person of the Dean of Durham, into a duck pond (mistaking him for the Bishop), the chapels were full of their friends learning to read, to write and to speak in public. The Free Churches in particular, filled an educational and a political and a time-killing vacuum. The working man – who really was the non-working man – either had to take advantage of what limited facilities the chapel had to offer, or do without altogether. With the rise to 'respectability' of the Labour Party and the introduction of the 1944 Education Act, the church began to lose several footholds at once.

The trouble was that Christians had deceived themselves into believing that one of the footholds had been a religious one, and that they had been speaking to the soul of man. This was far from being the case.

This influence of church and chapel also coincided with the impressive church-going habits of the middle classes. The pulpit ministries played a great role in the life of Britain and the United States, and crowds flocked every week, twice a Sunday, to hear a Dale of Carr's Lane, or a Fosdick of Riverside. Many of the churches in which they congregated were set in the middle of the cities, and they were packed to the doors and galleries. This phenomenon gave rise in Britain to a mistake in strategy on the part of the same churches after the second world war. As I myself have suffered from its consequences I naturally have a masochistic interest in spelling it out.

Many of the city churches which existed before the last war had been built as the result of the edifice-fixation which equated mission with buildings. Vast auditoriums, serving as centres for preaching and worship, were erected in the heart of our cities and towns. They were geographically placed in areas where there were large concentrations of population, areas which in recent times have been given over almost entirely to office blocks and shopping centres. Although these communities were more stratified than they are today, the predominant, residential grouping came from the artisan class.

This created an illusion that the full churches were serving the immediate neighbourhood and that the neighbourhood was coming to

church. This was far from being the case. As recently as 1938 George MacLeod left a successful parish ministry in Govan, Glasgow, in order to think through such a problem. His congregation came from all over the city, and other parts of Scotland besides, but only a tiny handful from the parish itself.

CLERICAL ERROR

In Britain after the war, churches up and down the land were faced with the spectacle of bombed buildings and the movement of population out into the new housing areas on a city's boundaries. It seemed to be the most natural reaction to this trend to say, 'We must do as before, and build where the people are.' The mistake was to forget that the people they were intending to follow had never really been all that interested in the church as such, except for those occasions when it had had practical aid to offer in the fields of education, politics, and soup kitchens.

And so we witnessed the erection of a multiplicity of edifices, often with the aid of government war-damage subsidies. With the exception of those in parts of Scotland many have remained nearly empty ever since. The only thing that has increased has been the cost of keeping them in some sort of repair and respectability.

Nor has the situation been eased by the action which was hailed, rather pathetically, at the time, as a victory for ecumenism. Certain Free Church Federal Councils, like my own in Bristol, agreed to erect only one Free Church on each housing estate, and this was decided in relation to denominational strength as it had existed in the city before the war. The Presbyterians, with only two buildings in the city before the war, one of which was destroyed, were granted permission to build on one estate. We accepted the offer.

In practice this meant that we placed ourselves in the midst of a people of whom the vast majority never had had a close attachment to the church where only two out of an initial population of 10,000 had been to a presbyterian church and where 99.99 per cent had not asked for a church in the first place.

Of course, if the church was to wait to be invited into every area before she could do the job, she would wait for a very long time. She has a task laid upon her which cannot linger for any man's prior summons. But the point is that the task of mission must not in each case be equated with the immediate construction of buildings. If David

Livingstone had been burdened from the start with a large sanctuary to maintain, a boiler to coax, and a garden to tend, Stanley would not have had so far to travel. But neither, for that matter, would the gospel.

And so in the Britain of the late forties and early fifties structures, both of building and ministry, were imposed upon whole sections of a community, which had never asked for them in the first place. Coupled with this, people in these communities were much more mobile than they had ever been before. If they did happen to have any loyalty to a church they were able to travel back there with consummate ease; the whole city was now a parish. But on the other hand, the motor-car was more likely to take the place of any religious habits which remained.

Despite the frustrating lessons there for all to see, the same pattern continues with remarkable regularity. Some local church authorities are more aware of this than others, but are then faced with another dilemma. This is the problem of land shortage. Today, whole plots of land can be gobbled up by interested parties well in advance of any buildings, and so it is not always practical to wait for a congregation to gather of itself and then request a site. It could be too late. But even this quandary could be dealt with more realistically than at present.

TREAD MILL

As a young minister, straight out of college, I was faced with just such a 'planted' new building. It was at the centre of an almost new, definitely monochrome, council house estate. It consisted of a modern sanctuary, a large hall, a small hall, and ancillary rooms. I did not question for one moment that it was our job to get people into it, and, especially, into the pews. By dint of very hard work, the small congregation, my colleagues, and myself managed, for about ten years, to present a reasonable-looking show to the rest of the Church and the community. (3)

The main emphasis had to be on youth; their parents were too hard a prospect. So it was that, in a day before the commercial enterprises really got into their stride, we made a concerted drive to provide an attractive meeting place for the young. Conjoined with coffee bars, discotheques, football teams and the modern passion play which we wrote called, *A Man Dies* (4) a creditable show was maintained for a number of years. I would also argue that it was more than just a show, but it did not result over all those years in any real increase in membership. It was, and is, very hard work. Jones and Wesson (5) have

62

summed it all up quite admirably,

'Go to the post-war council estate and look at its churches. God, how forlorn they are! Youth organisations dominate them and Sunday Schools are big. But it is all so rootless, and the kids are fed up with 'religion' when they are twelve. A few women come to church, and fewer men . . . The estate has already broken the hearts of many clergy. It will break many more. They never stay long.'

'Youth organisations dominate them'. With a club sometimes numbering a membership of 700 this, I suppose, was certainly true and still is, in our case. But what was, and is, the alternative? How could a small congregation have paid for the upkeep of such buildings, for plant which was far in excess of their needs? If it had not been for gradually working out a progressive partnership between ourselves and the statutory authority, in this case the Local Education Authority, and benefiting by grants for maintenance in respect of the youth service we provide, we would have been bankrupt long ago.

But what of those colleagues who either do not have this option open to them or do not have the flair – and why should they? – for this kind of work? For them life is one headache after another, and depends on keeping a building open and a handful of folk happy.

In addition to this, many congregations have to send contributions to central funds for the paying of ministerial stipends. These are usually assessed according to the number of members on the role and sometimes on a proportion of church income as well. So it is that the needs of a building and the requirements of ministerial maintenance often result in a situation of incredible frustration for the minister and members. It is not altogether a burlesque to say that such a congregation has to spend its time raising money to keep the ministry going so that the minister may help the congregation to concentrate on its task of raising money to keep the building going within which money can be raised to keep the ministry going! And when they are faced with seemingly no escape from this kind of treadmill, is it little wonder that many ministers have got out?

'It will break many more. They never stay long'. It is not surprising that, once out, and breathing the heady air of freedom and seeing the possibility of a man's life again, they have determined to stay out. What is doubly sad, is that in several cases the break is made even more complete. They also opt out of the worshipping community altogether, or rather never opt 'in', wherever they happen to settle.

Is there any point in looking for a solution to this problem from the inside? The answer is definite where the 'way out' radical boys are concerned. It is 'No'. We are informed that the only way now left is that of revolution as opposed to evolution. It is no use thinking that we can tinker with the structure of the church as it has developed, or failed to develop, over the centuries. She is dying. The pity is that before her final spasm she will have had more needless time, talent and money spent on trying to keep her alive. But unless she is left to suppurate on the side-lines, the mission of God will be held back. Far from the church being a sign and a foretaste of the kingdom, she is more akin to a sign and a foretaste of death, from which there is no resurrection.

The trouble with such a view is the unsatisfactory alternatives that are offered, if any are, to the church even as she is. Such critics cannot escape the fact that some kind of structure is necessary. And in the process of attempting to create a more viable form there is no reason why they should not come up against the problem of institutionalism which they hoped they had left far behind. Their last state could so easily be worse than their first.

'A plea has to be entered here with those who are impatient of all organisation and to whom "structure" is something of a dirty word as though the only structure that could be envisaged were a cage. All institutions from a university to a family need a structure in order to ensure the freedom of their members to associate with one another and with others. The characteristic achievements of the modern world are based on a high degree of organisation, not on the lack of it.' (6)

The same author reminds us of the Archbishop of Canterbury's dictum: 'institutions must be something and individuals must be free.'

It would seem that some of those on the extreme left wing, in their attempts to be fair to individuals, are being very unfair to institutions. It is also very difficult to see how you can be fair to individuals unless you are tackling in a realistic way the institutions which influence them, and which should serve them.

A LOVE-HATE RELATIONSHIP

The church is not that bad. Indeed, it is probably a good deal better and more flexible than I have so far made it out to be. Apart from economic considerations I can see no compelling reason why I, for instance, should get out and work at my christian commitment within

64

another context. Indeed I would find it very hard to do this apart from the church even as it is today.

I owe a great deal to the church and, in particular, to my own small denomination. Within it I have had the opportunity of knowing some of the kindest people I have ever met. My views on the amounts it pays its servants are apparent by this time, but they are amounts which are arrived at with scrupulous fairness in the light of the resources available. Other meagre resources are eaked out to provide pensions for retired ministers and homes for them to retire into. Many of the older men have shown me and my kind endless patience and consideration, when anywhere else we would have been ignored or patronised.

Surely, one would think, despite the church's faults, its old-fashioned appearance, its seeming rigidity, there is something here which could be worked on. Is it so bad? How can it be when it is a fact that all the congregations when lumped together form 'a major source of private development assistance to the developing nations with a significantly larger service budget than most of the United Nations development agencies combined.' (7) I cannot escape the fact that I owe my christian faith in great part to the church, and to the captive suburban church at that! Indeed it is hard to see from what other body or source I could have received the initial nourishment which I did receive, apart from my parents, and they received theirs in large part from the church. People like myself have a love-hate relationship with the church. She infuriates us, yet we cannot do without her. We would often like to leave her, but where else can we go?

When I think of the calibre of some of the men, ministerial and lay, which the institutional church can still throw up today, I am certainly less and less confident in thinking that I could do better on my own, or especially with fellow rebels.

I must also confess that the subjective experience of my original 'call' to the ministry is something I cannot lightly shake off. My conviction still is that it committed me, for better or for worse, to the church. And in the years since that traumatic experience I have not doubted that such a 'claim' actually took place, and that it still re-presents itself today from time to time with undiminished strength.

Then there is the empirical evidence provided by the history of the church. If I am deluded about my 'call' then at least I am in very good company. Church history, not to mention biblical history, offers thousands of examples of people who have been convinced of the reality of the claim upon them. Their enormous number is no more a proof of the validity of their experience than is my solitary conviction. But if I provide ripe material for the psychiatrist, it is at least a little comforting to know that I am not alone. But it is this kind of conviction, conjoined with the affection that many of us do have for the household of faith, that adds to the present pain and frustration.

One of the encouraging signs is the growing number of voices clamouring for constructive change, voices which are no longer seemingly crying in a wilderness. The rest of this essay will simply try to add one more bleep to the rising crescendo.

RE-STRUCTURING THE CHURCH FOR MISSION

This, of course, is one of the 'in' phrases amongst ecumaniacs and the rest. But it is a good, comprehensive phrase. It is a reminder of the need for change, and also the reason for that change. The work of mission is the reason for the church's existence, and she must be organised solely with that end in view. But a word of clarification first:

'We must, however, recognise the important distinction between mission and missions – mission is the action of God in which the church participates; missions are particular forms, related to specific times, places or needs, of that participation. To accept this is to accept a revolution in thinking about the church and mission – one can no longer think of the church supporting missions, as an occasional activity, since the church is the church only in so far as it participates in the mission of God.' (8)

The sentence, 'Mission is the action of God in which the church participates', is the key to an understanding of how the church can share openly and joyfully, in the process of secularisation. The latter is not divorced from the activity of God and we would add that it is meaningless when divorced from the christian faith.

'The task of the christian mission is to help men to open their eyes to the Christ who is already their Saviour. We are not called to a pagan country as missionaries because Christ is not there – he is there. We are not summoned to minister to the pagan because he is without Christ. The very summons comes from the Christ who is already there, who has dwelt with the person long before we ever arrived.' (9)

To argue this way is not to deny the need for a worshipping fellowship and bases from which that fellowship operates. It is to
66

remind ourselves that perhaps our primary task is not to bring people from one area of relationships to another within the church building; rather is it to try to reveal to them, where they are, and in the relationships which they are already enjoying, the ever present king of kings and lord of lords.

If the church is to be adequately prepared to participate in the mission of God she has to be more flexible than at present; perhaps to operate from fewer, but firmer, bases; and definitely to forget any idea of engaging with the world on a solitary denominational ticket.

It is said that the church in Britain is faced today with a missionary situation akin to the missionary challenge of the nineteenth century. There is truth in this, but the parallels are by no means exact. We do not start from scratch, as far as plant and congregations are concerned. Our re-structuring will involve the re-deployment and, perhaps, the dismissing of manpower. It will involve the greater planning of the use or non-use of buildings. But at least we have these things available for reorganising or dispensing with. Our being confronted by, and our co-operation wtih, the movement of secularisation will involve a complete re-training of personnel, but at least we have got the men to retrain. In addition, there is still a considerable residue of good-will in the attitudes of people to the church. They may think we are basically irrelevant to the modern scene, perhaps rather quaint, but they quite like to know we are around. This is the kind of capital we are living on at the moment. It is not earning much interest, but it is just possible that it could be put to better use.

PAST AND PRESENT

Again today's situation is different because of the distinction that has already been made between mission and missions, but there are many lessons still to be learned from the experience of the old missionary movement and especially the process begun at the International Missionary Conference held at Edinburgh in 1910, and its aftermath. At that time many missionaries and others had been feeling the frustration which has its counterpart today. The forces of paganism were just as daunting as the modern forces of secularism. The cry was taken up, 'evangelisation of the world in this generation.' but people acknowledged that it would remain only a cry unless denominational duplication could be brought to an end. The sheer wastage of resources, not to mention the impression of a divided gospel, was a scandal.

By 1935 that remarkable man, J.H. Oldham, who was made

secretary of the Continuing Committee, was asking whether the time had come for the mission agencies and the churches to begin to look together at the total needs of a given area and to make all their work contributory to a common objective approved by all. . . . 'What is required is a new habit of mind which thinks instinctively in terms not of a particular church or mission, but of the christian enterprise as a whole in the area in question.'

Today, people are saying the same things about the role of the church in the west, and at New Delhi, where the International Missionary Council and the World Council of Churches became one body, the concept of 'Joint Action for Mission' was emphasised very strongly.

The Nottingham Faith and Order Conference, meeting in 1964, in looking at the british scene, coined the phrase, 'areas of ecumenical experiment'. This described areas where there was already co-operation of a kind which went beyond what was then considered normal. Since 1964 the number of such areas has increased, and as a result, a memorandum from the Department of Mission and Unity of the British Council of Churches was presented to that council in August 1969, outlining how such places could be officially designated. The definition of such is areas where 'under responsible authority, certain denominational traditions are suspended for a period in order that new patterns of worship, mission and ministry can be undertaken.' (10)

At the time of writing, this report is about to be received into several denominational pipe-lines. It has given more than a glimmer of hope to many people, including myself.

Finally, attention should be drawn to the Uppsala Assembly's call in 1968 to the churches to search out in a new way the 'priority situations for mission', and to ask in each area, 'Are we totally structured for mission?'

'It called for a congregational commitment to mission in it's neighbourhood, for teams to undertake specific tasks, and for new structures of global co-operation which would make the resources of the whole church available for the use of the whole church — their deployment being determined not by historic relationships or traditional procedures, but by need . . . it is a fact that Christians are more and more inclined to feel that traditional confessional loyalties ought not to count against the claims of obvious immediate duty. If the denominations lag behind, so much for them. Those who see the job to be done will go ahead and do it, tarrying for none.' (11)

So from within the present church things are beginning to stir, and the movement towards change and re-structuring is already gaining momentum. Participants in this already have a certain ruthlessness of aspect, as if to warn all the (still considerable) forces of reaction not to stand in the way any longer. 'If the denominations lag behind, so much the worse for them, '. . . though one is tempted to add, from a practical point of view, 'If they do lag behind, who is going to pay the rebels then?' However, I think the tide that has begun to rise will be too strong in the end for the laggards. They will either have to swim with it, or be swept far out of sight.

Of course this is not to ignore the more pedestrian efforts that are now taking place to bring Anglicans and Methodists, Presbyterians and Congregationalists, and others, together. Both processes are not mutually exclusive. Indeed Newbigin in the same article claims that it was only after the churches in South India had tackled the major questions of Faith and Order that they were then enabled to feel their way towards more flexible and 'local' forms of church life.

This is salutary advice, but it should not blind us to the fact that there are urgent questions of 'local' structure which have to be tackled immediately without waiting for any man. Already the unity talks in Britain have a weary look about them, and the thrust needs to come from a new direction if even they are to gain fresh momentum.

SPECULATION

Well, what kind of church are we hoping will be fashioned out of the ashes of the old? And can it ever be a reality?

The Administrative Committee of the British Council of Churches, in a paper of June 1969 dealing with Churches and Population Movements, suggests:

'When considering capital expenditure and its usage, it is important to consider the best way of providing for all that the work and mission of the churches requires, planning it as a whole, but with flexibility . . . Although it is recognised that each major area may require a central "shrine" in the form of a church building, provisions for worship do not, in all cases, require a separate, detached building in its own grounds but could be incorporated in blocks of flats or offices, and most of the space could be usable for

69

other purposes. In planning the plant needed by the church care needs to be taken to relate it to the other social habits and activities of the community.'

'Each major area may require a central "shrine" ', says the report. This might well be the case. Of course the size of the area will vary according to a variety of factors; there could possibly be three such shrines in a more traditional church-going suburban area in order to get the people in, although it might be a healthier tactic to keep some of them out!

But in a housing estate of less than 17,000, there should be only room for one shrine instead of the usual two to five competing, and three-quarter empty sancturaries. In some city centres one shrine will be more than adequate, and who knows, the existing cathedral or central hall might fit the bill.

We have to realise that the local congregation no longer needs the buildings of former years. Of course quite a deal of plant will always be needed. Blow up your cathedral and you may well have to erect a marquee in the deanery garden the next day – provided the dean had also been blown up with the cathedral! But with the presence of a large and functional central shrine, the Christians of an area will have to plan accordingly for what their real needs are. Each enclave will no longer require its own building. One of the functions of the shrine would be that of 'worship centre', and this alone should relieve local groups from the present chore of thinking they have to maintain two services on a Sunday, each with five hymns and a sermon to boot.

There ought to be alternative choices of forms of worship, whereas the present choice offered by St. Balderdash's at the corner of Holy Thingummybob on the Square is limited indeed and wouldn't it be welcome if, instead of singing five hymns at every service, we had the choice in our region of a Quaker type service if we happened to feel that way?

But this is simply to engage in too much speculation. And indeed it has been adequately speculated upon in recent books, such as 'Towards a Radical Church' (12) by Jones & Wesson and (almost similarly titled), 'Toward a Radical Church' (13) by Joseph C. McLelland. However, the exciting fact is that such ideas are not entirely speculative, but are beginning to be actualised in particular situations. Those who would like to examine one particular situation where re-structuring on a regional basis is beginning to look a distinct possibility are referred to the booklet, 'Structuring the Church for Mission' (14). It is a comprehensive report concerning the church in the region of Teeside with radical proposals for re-structuring the same. The exciting prospect is the favourable reception it seems to have been given by the ministers and clergy of the region.

Of course, the need for change should not apply only to buildings. It has to apply to the re-shaping of the body of believers themselves and in particular with that part of the body which is the special concern of this symposium — the ordained ministry.

PREACHER AND PASTOR

I said at the beginning that I was convinced that there was a role for the minister of word and sacraments, and we must examine this aspect more closely. I also said that that role was about to undergo trenchant change. I hope that what has already been said will have given some indication of why this has to be. The process of secularisation, the emphasis on the participation in the ongoing mission of God in the world, and the need for much reorganisation in relation to buildings, also presuppose changes in the traditional role of the ministry, if indeed they do not presuppose its disappearance altogether.

As we are mainly concerned with the particular role of the Free Church minister, for convenience sake we can sub-divide this into two parts: Preacher and Pastor.

THE MINISTER AS PREACHER

The Pauline injunction was, 'How can they hear without a preacher?' to which the rueful addendum today might be, 'How can they preach without a congregation?' This seems to be a difficulty which many of the manuals on preaching conveniently ignore. Even some comparatively modern ones make the assumption that there will be people present to be preached at.

However, a classic like H.H. Farmer's 'Servant of the Word' (15) can speak to the modern predicament as effectively as it spoke when it was first published.

'(Christian revelation) all begins in an Event, or rather The Event, God's Event ... From the beginning, then, Christianity, being concerned with The Event which by definition has no parallel, God being agent in it as He is not in other happenings, was committed to preaching, to proclamation. Whoso said Christianity, said preaching.

There was no choice between that and absolutely ceasing to be, with not the least chance of ever occurring again.' (pp 18-19).

To agree with such a definition is not to commit oneself to being a pulpiteer or to spend one's days in writing two sermons for a Sunday. It is proclamation of the event which matters, and this is the responsibility of the whole church. Farmer maintains,

'Furthermore it is a fact . . . that if preaching is not accompanied by some participation in men's personal situations and needs, it loses much of its power to convince. The two types of activity should be held firmly together, as they are in the gospels. It is a perfect illustration of the principle, "these ought you to have done, and not to leave the other undone." ' (p.24).

If Christianity is preaching – 'proclamation' is a better word – then it is the responsibility of the whole church. And the whole body is better placed to engage in realistic 'participation in men's personal situations and needs' far more than, for instance, the parson by himself. But if the whole body takes up its responsibility for proclamation of the event to the world, I can see the role of the minister becoming more, not less, in demand. He, at this point, could really come into his own as a specialist in the Ephesian epistle's sense of being the supporter of the rest of the body in their ministry of proclamation. 'To some he gave the power to guide and teach his people' (Ephesians 4, J.B. Phillips). Farmer quotes Herrmann as saying long ago that the minister's 'most distinctive function – for it is one which no one else in the Christian community can discharge – is to produce, preserve, and utilise a sound theology.'

Now the producing and utilising of such a theology need not be for pulpit purposes at all. It should be available for the providing of information and theological insight for the use of the other members of the body to enable them to participate the more effectively in mission to the world.

A man I know recently resigned from the ministry because he had some christological difficulties and felt he could no longer occupy a pulpit. There have been others like him. But the pity is he equated coming out of the pulpit with coming out of the ministry. He probably would have been an excellent minister if he had come out of the pulpit and stayed in the congregation, sharing with them his problems and his vision.

72

This emphasis on the minister as trainer and provider, rather than as pulpiteer, will demand a higher standard of theology, not a lesser one. Many a cleric still gets away with murder in the pulpit where he is not open to answering questions or, for that matter, to the real needs of the people. But in this new setting he would be in constant demand by the congregation, or group of congregations, which he served. His theological knowledge, combined with a sympathetic understanding of the structures under which people live, work and play today, plus a thorough training in modern skills of group training, and the like, could see the emergence of a smaller, but highly qualified, class of professional man and woman.

Lesslie Newbigin has written:

'God's unique and saving revelation of himself in Jesus Christ enables men to interpret what is happening to them and to respond to the calling of God in the midst of the life of the world . . . What is required is an understanding of the relation between what God has done — uniquely and finally — in Christ and what he is doing in the life of mankind as a whole, an understanding which will enable Christians to communicate the gospel in words and patterns of living which are in accordance with what God is doing, and is calling men to do, in their secular life.' (16)

This is quoted by J.G. Davies in 'Worship and Mission' and he comments,

'If this be the function of the sermon, to enable the hearers to appreciate the meaning of the gospel in terms of their life in the world, then we have to confess that this lies outside the competence of many preachers. When life was a unity, when the horizon was that of a closely knit community, the parson could know his people and their problems, in work and leisure, and could speak to their situation. Today, because of the phonomenon of differentiation, he can no longer be familiar in depth with the living issues and the circumstances of work of the many social groups that compose modern society. His sermon may therefore assume a docetic character, in that it does not serve the incarnation of the kerygma in the daily lives of the congregation and cannot do so because he is not a universal know-all. Hence the sermon as an authoritative monologue is suspect at the present time. The choice however is not solely between silence and mouthing words that are irrelevant; it should be possible to replace monologue by dialogue. It should be possible to prepare the sermon by means of team work, so that through joint participation the concrete situations of the contemporary world, known to the laity from within, may be taken into account. In this way there can be hope that the gospel may be declared in the thought-forms of the congregation; in this way the sermon may assume a missionary dimension.' (17)

With this I heartily agree. But it demonstrates all the more the need for a highly skilled group of professionals trained to 'produce, preserve, and utilize a sound theology.' This, of course, does not mean one to every enclave of Christians; they probably would best be congregated in teams, based on the central shrine of an area or region.

Paradoxically, the high standard of training and skill required for such professionals could result at first in even fewer candidates presenting themselves for the ministry than at the moment. But this would be a healthier state than the present tendency to lower the standards in order to scrape enough 'preacher' types together to meet the imagined needs of dwindling congregations. And accompanied by the re-structuring of buildings and financial resources (and ecumenical experiments are very closely allied to economical experiments), the small band of new professionals should be paid a possible starting salary of £2,000 a year, if not more.

THE MINISTER AS PASTOR

When we look back it is easy to see why the parson took upon himself the role of pastor, the visitor of the flock and the counsellor of the distressed. His economic and educational status, and his freedom from the drudgery of the working man's day, gave him the ability and opportunity to do all this if he was so disposed. It could be argued that, because of the structures of society, no other option was open to him. To have attempted a more democratic, non-directive approach would have been to land himself in a lunatic asylum or to his being despised by the very people he was seeking to draw into areas of mutual responsibility. It would have been greeted by a surprise akin to Attila's taking a vote amongst the Huns whether they wished to invade Gaul or not.

But today there are others in a congregation who could be, and often are, better pastors than the minister. A young, but not inexperienced minister, asked recently why he should be expected to counsel the dying when there were at least three people in his small congregation who could do it better than he. A university lecturer told me how in college he found himself in the role of counsellor, sometimes almost to several students at once. Yet he found such individual counselling an impossibility. For one thing it was spiritually draining and the rest of his work suffered. But for it to be effective it had to be shared with other colleagues and, for that matter, other students. Thereby the person was able to have the best help.

Real pastoral counselling and concern ought to be a corporate, shared, affair. But the minister still assumes it is his role alone, and thus he suffers double frustration as he has fewer and fewer people upon whom he can exercise this role and discovers that, amidst the other pressures of modern society, his words of cheer and wisdom are by no means adequate or even appropriate.

But what a picture of the task as it has been whittled down through the years! The minister is a man who is expected to preach, to visit, to counsel, but he lives in a society which does not come to hear him preach, does not require him to visit, and, if it needs counselling, will go elsewhere for it. And if this is how the church will continue to view him, then the calibre of candidates as well as their quantity, must decrease very rapidly.

The church today must pay much more attention to the insights of educationists and sociologists in their approach to problems of community development and the encouragement of group participation. I am thinking in particular of the work of T.R. Batten (18) in this country and Earl C. Kelley in the United States. (19)

What Batten has to say about the role of the worker in the group could almost be transferred to a possible role for the ministry today,

'The worker who uses the non-directive approach does not attempt to decide for people, or to lead, guide, or persuade them to accept any of his own conclusions about what is good for them. He tries to get them to decide for themselves what their needs are: what if anything, they are willing to do to meet them; and how they can best organise, plan, and act to carry their project through. Thus he aims at stimulating a process of self-determination and self-help, and he values it for all the potential learning experiences which participation in this process provides. He aims to encourage people to develop themselves, and it is by thinking and acting for themselves, he believes, that they are most likely to do so. Moreover, the outcome will usually be a project designed to produce some change for the better in people's lives. Thus two kinds of betterment result, and change in people and change in their environment go hand in hand.' (20)

75

It would be hard to find a fuller description of the role of the minister as some of us would like to see it develop in the future. And who would deny that the presence of a highly-trained group of specialists, grounded in christian theology, would have a cumulative effect on the life of the church which would the better equip it for its task of participation in the mission of God?

Of course the non-directive approach is one which is alien to many a parson by nature of his training and outlook. Anything which threatens to remove him from a fast-shrinking stage is simply calculated to add to his bewilderment. Strange this, when such an approach can also be justified on theological grounds.

Norman Pittenger, writing about the way in which God is at work in the world says,

> 'I should be prepared to say that the non-God world has a radical freedom which God himself must and does accept. That is how things are; and theologically we might phrase it by saying that such is how God wants things to be. His accomplishments in the world, with the ultimate victory of his good over everything, are to be achieved not by denial of but through those decisions in freedom. Because this is how things are, the working "through decisions in freedom" requires a subtlety of divine operation rather than a direct and immediate manipulation of created or creaturely occasions.' (21)

One is not being irreverent when one is tempted to say; 'Well, what's good enough for God ought to be good enough for us.' One could almost talk of 'God's non-directive approach'. Certainly the way in which Jesus dealt with people and situations is an illustration of this very point. The recognition scene at Caesarea Philippi, is a supreme example of Jesus' bringing people to make the discovery for themselves concerning the nature of his own person. And when they had made that discovery at the cross, they were more likely to understand it than if it had been presented to them as a take-it-or-leave-it fact.

Is it not too much to hope that those who feel themselves called to the ministry of word and sacrament may recall how in that whole process of being 'claimed' by another, their integrity and freedom were respected at every point by the 'claimer'? And that in turn they may try to deal just as graciously with those they have been called to serve, (the body of Christ) that the members too may behave similarly towards the world as they seek to participate with God in his mission to that world?

It might be worth a try!

1. World Council of Churches Conference on Church and Society, Official Report, paras. 110-112.
2. *The Future of Religion,* Watts. New Thinkers Library 1969. p25.
3. See *Odds Against* (SCM) and *Odds Against Evens* (Westminster Press).
4. Darton Longman and Todd. 1964.
5. *Towards a Radical Church,* (Epworth Press), pp10-11.
6. Kathleen Bliss. op.cit.60.
7. Report by Dr Richard Dickinson published by the World Council of Churches, 1968.
8. *Worship and Mission* by J.G. Davies. SCM. 1966.
9. *God's Mission and Ours,* by E.L. Smith. (Quoted by J.G. Davies ibid, 30.)
10. *The Designation of Areas of Ecumenical Experiment.* A report to the B.C.C. by the Department of Mission and Unity. 1969.
11. Lesslie Newbigin, writing in *International Review of Mission,* XXX,XXX, Jan.1970.
12. Epworth Press, 1970.
13. Saint Andrew Press, 1970.
14. Belton Books, 181 Creighton Avenue, London N.2.
15. Nisbet, 1941.
16. *The Relevance of Trinitarian Doctrine for Today's Mission.*
17. op.cit., 134.
18. *The Non-Directive Approach in Group and Community Work,* O.U.P.1967.
19. *The Workshop Way of Learning.*
20. op.cit., 11-12.
21. *Goodness Distorted, p32, Mowbrays 1970.*

BEYOND THE CRISIS

by Alec Gilmore

So far we have looked at the radical and iconoclastic approach to church and ministry which concludes that within a decade we may not even know what is meant by full-time service in the ministry. We have looked at a theological defence of that same ministry developed in relation to church, Word and sacrament. We have had an account of the practical problems faced by one particular minister in a situation which was new enough, open-ended enough and untraditional enough to allow almost anything to happen, but which in the end shows up how strong is the grip of the traditional and 'what is expected' even there, and how difficult it is to be radical in one place while all around goes on as before. Are there any practical rays of hope we can offer in conclusion to those men who are still trying to make a go of the ministry either because they believe in it or they can do nothing else?

It's a pity that ministers tend to fall in one of two camps—either the disillusioned or the euphoric. A few years ago it was most refreshing to spend a week end in the home of one of my colleagues in an inner city area which was more black than white. The previous ministers had shouted louder and louder in the hope of drawing a congregation from further and further afield. This particular man had simply told his people that their mission field was on their doorstep. It created for him a difficult job, started, and in the end saved, only because he himself was willing to do a fair amount of the work. He saw all the weaknesses of the church, the ministry and denomination. But he still believed in it all and was only anxious to apply himself to both the difficulties and the opportunities that they offered.

Since then I have met many radicals crying out in disillusionment that the whole thing was doomed, and I have met many conservatives who are sure that the radicals are sick and that nothing is wrong. Having now therefore looked at the strengths and weaknesses of the ministry as it presents itself today at the ground level, two tasks remain to be done. One is to see the minister's crisis as part of a much wider crisis. The other is to try to spot one or two growing points for the minister, whatever his situation happens to be. We must take them in order.

CRISIS IN SOCIETY

If the crisis in the ministry is to be seen in perspective, then the first thing to be said is that it is part of a wider crisis in society as a whole.

78

The ministerial office may not be what it used to be, but neither is that of the teacher, the doctor, the dentist, the local government officer and a host of other people. Nor is it only a matter of pay.

It reminds me of a minister who moved to one of the 'plums' of his own denomination and was reported after only two years to be 'not very happy' in the church, to which a poorer colleague remarked, 'Well, he won't mind being unhappy there.' But he did. And so would most of his brethren.

Again it is often argued that the ministry is not bad for the first fifteen to twenty years, but that men then become aware of the weaknesses of the profession in middle life. What perhaps is sometimes missed in this connection is the emergence of a new elite. The top of the social ladder used to be the educated person who was usually to be found in the professions. The top is probably still the educated person, but today you are just as likely to find him in business with all the appurtenances of an expense account, the firm's car and an infra-structure of staff which gives him both time and opportunity for all kinds of things which are less readily available to the professional who may well be working single-handed.

For the ministry however there are three aspects of a crisis in society which have contributed to his own crisis; some of these have been touched on earlier and will not need much elaboration. First, the changes in the social services have left the minister without a role, as earlier contributions have amply illustrated. Pastoral work, once the shepherd's care of the community, has tended to become the visitation of the congregation and the sorting out of petty squabbles.

Secondly, changes in education have produced an age of questioning. Experts may still exist but they are few and far between. In the social sciences they are almost non-existent and if a minister has this gift he is more likely to be outside the ministry manning the social services and not living in a vicarage.

The minister's field of activity has been narrowed down, and even then his territory has been invaded. When pushed to its ultimates the minister's role today has to do with the three great moments of birth, marriage and death, but he can no longer dogmatise even on these. The problems of birth, as far as the minister is concerned, are problems of the meaning of life rather than problems of obstetrics, but nowadays this also requires attention to matters of family planning, abortion and possibly mercy-killing, on which the minister qua minister is hardly competent to pronounce and on which he may not even be consulted.

If he is, he is likely to be quite the least important member of the team, and others will be listened to much more readily. When it comes to marriage, apart from the business of performing the ceremony, people are much more likely to turn to their solicitor or the local Marriage Guidance Counsellor, and when it comes to death there is probably more active study of bereavement among psychiatrists than there is among clergy.

The minister's answer to this is the reconstruction of a new theology. He has to take the new situations, developments and changed relationships within society and re-discover his own role by re-discovering the place and action of God in contemporary events. But alas, this is the one situation for which he was never trained. Like the child who was taught the catechetical questions to the catechetical answers the minister was taught the theological problems and the theological answers. What he was not taught was how to work out the answers for himself and his people once the problems changed their form.(1)

Thirdly, changes in communication have robbed the minister of his 'pulpit'. In common with the politicians' hustings and possibly with the W.E.A.'s lecturers platform, there is a rapidly diminishing number of people who will sit for even as long as twenty minutes and listen to a man pour out his soul or parade his opinions, however moving the one or erudite the other, and if they do they will certainly want plenty of time afterwards to question him on what he said if not actually interrupt him in the middle. Caryl Micklem's distinction here between the crowd occasion and the group occasion is a very useful one, for most ministers are working with groups rather than with crowds and they are slower than university and college of education lecturers to change their patterns of communication, and the resistance may be greater. If people wanted the commodity, if there was no other way of obtaining it, even this would save the day for the pulpit. But this is not so; the commodity which people do want is a glimpse of eternity. They want to see beyond the supermarket and the superficial but they are turning to places other than the church and the pulpit for it.

Not all men who find their ministry in crisis are consciously aware of all these factors, and may indeed readily locate their troubles in other places such as economics or the buildings or the failure of the laity to take their duty seriously, but the total crisis cannot be understood unless it is seen against this background of society.

CRISIS IN THE CHURCH

In the last decade almost all the stress in the church has been on Christ the Servant, and Isaiah 53. Robin Sharp (2) sums it up by saying,

'...the dominant note of our thinking about the church today is service. This goes for Pope John, the Archbishop of Canterbury, Professor Hromadka, the Bishop of Woolwich (then John Robinson), the New Delhi Assembly, the S.C.M. and just about every church statement one can think of...The church is to be present in the world and is to serve it...It's *raison d'etre* is in giving itself for the life of the world.'

Put the emphasis on the servant-church and the important thing is what the church has to give. The true church becomes the suffering church, the humiliated church and even the dying church. The purpose of the church and of the ministry is unitedly for the world and not for the church. The B.C.C. report stressed this point on sociological as well as theological grounds and saw the ministry as addressed not so much to individuals as to persons in community, where the appropriate 'image' is not 'rescue from the world' but 'leaven acting within the world'. (3) All this the minister shares with his congregation because he is a layman first and a minister second. This is all very well, but it has left many ministers increasingly puzzled. They know what to do as a member of the servant church, but are not sure what to do as the minister of the servant church. Answers along the line that they are there to equip the saints for their ministry, or that they are meant to be 'backroom boys' serving those members who are in the front line, are good scriptural and theological answers, but they tend to overlook some of the ministers' practical problems.

For example, if his church members take their mission as servants seriously, then they will spend more time in the world than they do in the church. Nothing wrong here, except that part of many a minister's support and strength have come from having a large, busy, thriving and active community around him. Once this begins to diminish in terms of man-hours spent at the church, or at the manse or in church administration, it is inevitable that it does something to the minister and to his own understanding of the role he has to play.

Furthermore, every church is made up of people who are able to go out into the community to fulfil their mission and of people who are not. Some of these are finding that they do not require many of the services that the church provides for them. Others, on the other hand, find that increasingly in a changing world they need the support of regular fellowship and corporate life in the kind of 'safe' environment that only the church can provide. They are in the church largely because they cannot cope with the world. If the trends of service continue, with mature and capable people finding their work increasingly outside the church, and the rest clinging more and more to the structures the minister must begin to ask himself what sort of role he has to fulfil.

Again if the most lively and able men are to begin to find their main mission in the world, their places in church administration will be taken more and more by less capable folk, and the minister will feel like Jerusalem after the exiles had gone. He is left with the poorest in the land.

Many ministers find certain other factors beyond their control. One is economics. Free Churches exist by voluntary contributions of their members and if the church declined below a certain number, then changes would have to be made. But in the present climate the size of the church may not be declining. It might even be increasing. The nature of the members' work in the community may be such as to require more ministerial time rather than less. On the other hand, the requirements for church buildings may be markedly less, and members who are for ever active in the community will question why they should contribute to the upkeep of premises which are scarcely needed, but yet which cannot always be disposed of. Contributions to the church may fall for other reasons. Once a man becomes involved in society there are all kinds of demands being made on his purse, and what he is able to give to the church is certainly likely to be pegged if not actually reduced. A lot of this will sort itself out in time, and to that extent the crisis may only be temporary, but it is no less a crisis whilst it lasts and it is much more of a crisis for the minister than it is for the members because his whole life is so bound up with it.

Another complication in the crisis which prevents a full grasping of the challenge is the tendency for polarisation. As long as the church went on steadily without noticeable change the church community didn't find it difficult to function as a unit. Once changes are proposed there is a tendency for the congregation to take up sides for and against. In the long run such tension can have a beneficial effect, for it is out of such tension that progress emerges. But it doesn't make things easier for the ministry in the present, for the minister is inevitably at the centre, torn between his desire to take sides according to his

82

convictions and the necessity he feels for holding the congregation together lest he should create further division.

Again, not every man who finds his ministry in crisis sees the crisis in the church this way, but these are nevertheless some of the factors that affect the ministry and make it impossible to deal with the ministry in isolation from the church.

CRISIS OF THE PERSON

The third thing to be said about the crisis in ministry is that it is part of a wider crisis in the minister's own life. Often a minister finds, like many members of his congregation, that he no longer believes in the way he used to believe. Certainty is not the god it once was, not even in the Roman Catholic Church on the one hand nor in the conservative evangelical world on the other, but all this means is that doubt is being entertained by more ministers, and often among those who by their training were brought up not to doubt, and thus brings its own difficulties. And even among men who have always lived with doubt on a number of issues, there seem to be more things to question than there used to be, and when a man has questioned nearly everything that exists he must inevitably look around him to see what he is left with.

There was a time when in such circumstances a minister would have turned to the theological experts, but today many of them are passing through the same kind of experience, as for instance when a group of Cambridge theologians publish a book like 'Soundings' and defend their title on the grounds that the time is not ripe for works of theological construction or reconstruction. 'It is a time for ploughing, not reaping,' they say; 'it is a time for making soundings, not charts or maps.' In the same volume, G.F.Woods explains why many thoughtful Christians of today find themselves bewildered in making moral judgments. They are, he says,

'like a navigator of a ship who has lost confidence in the reliability of his compass and the visibility or even dependability of the heavenly bodies and is puzzled to find that what he took to be alternative direction systems seem to be full of ingenuity and knowledge of the natural world but somehow unable to give any particular guidance about the particular course to follow on any particular occasion.' (4)

This is a very apt and telling description of how many a man feels in his ministry.

In some cases a man finds himself in an emotional crisis because he

83

has developed a more critical attitude to the things he is handling than he used to have. It used to be taken for granted that there was nothing much wrong with the Sunday services and all the church organisations and activities, and in this context it is interesting to note the way in which Ernest Marvin says that when he went to his church and found the premises he did not question for one moment that it was his job to get people into it. All they needed was a bit of improvement and modification. Better leadership was often looked upon as a panacea for all ills but rarely were the activities themselves submitted to closer scrutiny. The weapons for war needed oiling and polishing, but few people stopped to ask whether the weapons were obsolete.

Many illustrations of this could be given of which church buildings and church extension are but one. There are ministers who have seen the maintenance and extension of church premises not only as one of their main preoccupations but also as a measuring rod for their success. The man who could form new churches, secure land and erect halls and sanctuaries got a tremendous kick out of it. Of course, he may have been wrong but nobody told him so and there were many others quick to mark him out as a go-ahead minister.

If, in reply to this, it is argued that a man must learn to concentrate on his essential ministry, this only serves to raise the question as to what the essence of his ministry is. Is he just a preacher of the word and an administrator of the sacraments? The theological answer to this may well be that he is, and the theological analysis of this is provided elsewhere in this volume by Neville Clark where the ministerial function is related to the planning and execution of the church's worship and what arises from it. This is what the minister does qua minister. The rest he does qua layman, and qua layman he may be a youth leader or a Marriage Guidance Counsellor or a school teacher, or an organiser of old people's clubs or a dozen other things. It is a helpful and accurate answer and description, but the point to be made here is that the theological answer alone doesn't necessarily help the minister a great deal at the practical level, because he still has to determine his priorities and he may still suffer guilt or unrest if his mind directs him to abandon many of the facets on which his earlier ministry had been built. Another distinction which some ministers have found difficult to make and which has therefore produced tension is that between the pastor and the evangelist. 'We used to have a pool to fish in in those days,' said one of our elderly baptist ministers a few years ago, referring to the earlier days of his ministry at the beginning of the twentieth

century. What he meant was that the normal Sunday congregation was always far, far more than the total membership. That man could be a pastor to the flock and in preaching and ministering to them he was inevitably at the same time preaching and ministering to the unbeliever. He just didn't need to ask himself whether he was pastor or evangelist, for he couldn't be one and not the other.

Today, at least in baptist circles, a minister is lucky if his morning and evening congregations added together equal his total membership, and very few of them will be other than committed Christians. A subsidiary effect of this is that in exercising a pastoral ministry to them he will be given few natural opportunities of ministering to the unbeliever as his grandfather was. This is not to say he is not an evangelist, because his members are continually in need of evangelising, but it is to say that he is often forced to choose between staying inside the church with those there and going out to work among men and women in the community. Many men feel torn between the two.

One proposed solution already referred to is that ministers are to equip the saints for the work of the ministry, content themselves to be backroom boys serving the membership and giving them what they need for the task, so that they may go out to do the ministering to the community. There is much truth here, but it overlooks the fact that many men who are in the ministry, and certainly those who are in a state of crisis are just not backroom boy types. That's one thing. Another is that if you are to train a member for ministry and this means you need to have at least some experience of the situation in which he will work, ministers who are going to equip their members must themselves move freely in the world and play their part in it.

One more factor should be mentioned before we begin to see what a man can do with his crisis. All the emphasis on mission, service, outreach and community involvement are excellent from the point of view of the kingdom. So too is the kind of talk that refers to 'go structures' rather than 'come structures' to 'outreach' rather than 'in-drag'. If the whole of our local church could go this way the lot of many ministers would be eased. But it doesn't happen this way. For every one who goes out to fulfil his mission, two or three are likely to be left behind. Some of them are elderly, some are 'walking wounded'. They are the people who are unable to face up to life and who have retreated into the church because of it. They are the people who cannot stand the changes of the world and who have therefore taken refuge in the church on the principle that 'nothing changes here', themselves then taking good care that it doesn't. They demand that much of the usual church programme goes on, and whilst it goes on many ministers feel compelled to be involved in it. Here is just one more tension, resulting in the feeling that you can't do the work properly in either sphere.

Beyond this point the details of the crisis will vary from man to man and from situation to situation, and the value of a symposium of this kind is that it enables you to look at the situation through the eyes of different people. For my part, I see three problems to be faced and therefore three growing points for my ministry and for men in my situation. Every one of them is hopeful.

PREACHING AND THE CONDUCT OF WORSHIP

Preaching is such a personal thing that at times you feel it is impossible to say anything of yourself that will be of value to another preacher. Listening to sermons is such a personal thing that at times you feel as if there is no link at all between what you say and intend and what in fact happens in any member of the congregation. You can trail your coat and make outrageous statements and nothing happens. Then the bomb goes off in the most innocent of places.

Today the most popular thing to do with preaching is to lampoon it. You only need to see the little man in his pulpit or on television to want to feel sorry for him. He *must* be one of those who sees himself as safe and 'six feet above contradiction'. If you move the camera from the pulpit to the pew you expect them to be empty—unless of course it is a specially rigged service for television. Here is something left over from the age of dogmatism, a sea animal struggling to keep his end up on dry land. You can only pity him, etc. etc. etc. Add to this the more severe strictures which Caryl Micklem makes on the Call and the Lord's Supper and you begin to see how many preachers feel. Certainly this is how many people in the world react. Certainly there are many in every congregation who are there because they got into the habit when they were young rather than because they feel any burning desire to listen to what the preacher says, or have any great passion for worship. But it would be a mistake to see this as the whole story.

'Silly Little Man', a poem by Yvonne Abbatt (5), is a mildly humorous but sympathetic way of stating the problem. The point is that people do hear God and would like to hear more, but often feel that the preacher does not hear and therefore fails to help them as much as he might. But if people are hearing at all the preacher has his opportunity, and my own reading of the signs is that in order to seize it a preacher has to cultivate four attitudes, which are none of them new to preachers but which do seem to have gone underground in the last couple of generations or so at least.

First, he must cultivate *a realistic touch with the contemporary scene.* An earlier suggestion about praying with the newspapers is not as irrelevant as it may seem, and provided Neville Clark's warning is noted, there is nothing wrong with preaching round the newspapers as well. This has always been the mark of the prophet-preacher. Amos and Isaiah knew well enough what was happening around them and how people felt about it. Martin Luther knew the burdens his contemporaries carried. John Clifford, R.W.Dale and, in a different way, even Spurgeon, all had touch with their congregations, whilst Martin Luther King was almost the product of his social environment, but somewhere along the line many preachers have lost this touch with a resulting deadness for their congregations and a sense of ineffectiveness for themselves. Perhaps this is the most commonly heard criticism of preachers today—not that they are dull, nor even that they are long-winded, but that they are irrelevant.

If this is so preachers may take heart, for it is one of the things that can be remedied. One way is by getting the approach the right way round. Even many preachers who have plenty of contemporary references in their sermons begin with their sermons and pull in the contemporary reference. By this means, the starting point is still God, the church and the Bible. It is still the spiritual truths that are being given priority, and the events of the common life are being used in the worst sense simply as incidents to light up and illustrate what the preacher knows he is going to say anyway. His preaching will become relevant only if he can begin at the other end. If the world is to write the agenda for the church then the contemporary scene needs to set the subject for the sermon. Let God, the church and the Bible be related to that, not the other way round.

Nor is this just a matter of the old educational principle of beginning where people are and leading them on, nor of the old homiletical principle of beginning with the popular and familiar in order to arrest the audience's attention, before going on to meatier matters. Follow this principle and you lose the congregation once you get to the meat just as surely as you lose the children once you add the moral to the story. It is more far-reaching than either, because it requires the preacher to say to himself, 'Here is the contemporary

87

scene—what is God doing through it?' From there he may lead his congregation to judgment, to an experience of wonder, or to a change of heart, but he will be doing this in the events and not in relation to the events.

A teacher of infants said in my hearing that she didn't lay on formal acts of prayer or worship for her pupils, but when a child came into the classroom with a flower from the garden the act of worship was in the shared experience of wonder that teacher and pupil had together, and worship would only be destroyed if she were to say to the child, 'That's very nice— now shut your eyes and we'll say a prayer about it.' Too much of our preaching has come in this category where the contemporary scene has been used only as a means to getting at certain spiritual truths. Effective preaching and relevant preaching discovers new spiritual truths every week just by exploring the world.

Another way of securing relevance is by coming to terms with the fact that we live in an age of television. Books are irrelevant as far as the masses of people are concerned. Very many of them never hold a hard-back book from one year to another, and what many of them term books the minister would probably still refer to as magazines. The fact that the minister can still live in a world of books as much as he does is only evidence of the middle-class nature of almost all church communities.

A personal confession may underline the point. My training took place just before the advent of television. The diligent minister was the man who surrounded himself with books and if he had dared to have as much as a radio in his study he would have wanted to hide it when his members and colleagues called on him. If he were a lark he would rise at 6 and do at least an hour's reading before breakfast, and if he were a nightingale he would go to his study when he got in from his evening meetings and stay there till midnight. I happened to be the nightingale and so... I still cannot sit up watching the late-night television shows without the feeling that I am either indolent or lacking in will power. Yet I know that it is here that I can best be in touch with the world of my people, and it is here (notably on certain late night programmes) that I can find all the raw material for the best kind of theological thought and preaching.

Similarly, I was always taught that a free evening was an occasion for an extra couple of hours in the study— reading! Watching *Z-Cars* or *Coronation Street* could only be a concession to the weakness of the flesh—yet here again are popular aspects of life which require some

88

theological comment if they are to be more than merely entertainment. We shall say something later about helping people pastorally to see something of the significance of what they are doing. Here it is worth pausing to point out the opportunity preaching offers for helping people to see the significance of what they are looking at.

There is one crucial theological question to be asked by every preacher as he gazes at the world of his people: what is God doing through this? If this is asked, say, of *Coronation Street* then it seems to me that here is a programme which is no longer centred in the pub (which of itself has been sufficient to put off many nonconformists) but is centred in personal relationships. What is important is that people meet– they quarrel, they gossip, they criticise, they make it up, they sacrifice, they forgive, they dream dreams and see visions. All the stuff of the life is here and all the content of the christian gospel is to be found there, but thousands of people see it week after week and they never see beyond the pint. Nothing new here. Most people in Palestine in the time of Jesus never saw beyong the cripples, and the Scribes, and the Law. The gospel narratives are just full of story after story similar to the stories of *Coronation Street*. What made the incidents was what Jesus saw in them and what he made of them. Sermons that would deal with such subjects as meeting, forgiveness and reconciliation need to grow out of this kind of soil. The preacher certainly must have his own basic and theological sights set right, but that doesn't mean that he has to parade those sights in front of his congregation. Let the congregation be shown the building, not given an account of how we put up the scaffolding. Similar lines could be adopted with *Z-Cars, Softly, Softly* and many other programmes with this human touch.

If a preacher is in an urban area he can go further. There are plays and films that the local press will be writing about and his people will be going to see. These require more than a literary critic, they require a theological critique. Not, perhaps, as a regular event because the preacher fills a different role from the journalist. Nevertheless, if all his people are going off to see *Dr. Zhivago* and the preacher ignores all the theological issues such a book raises then he can only do so at his peril. *Waiting for Godot, Look Back in Anger, Hair,* (to mention only three) all give similar openings. Some plays and films lend themselves to this better than others and the man turning to this field for the first time will be wise to paddle rather than to wade, and even then in shallow and placid waters, but there is a new note of relevance here waiting to be seized.

Time spent in this way, coupled with the theological thinking that goes with it, can give the preacher an opportunity and a relevance that puts new meaning into his work. The global village is on a 19-inch screen! People need help in interpreting it.

Secondly, he needs to learn to think in pictures rather than in ideas. Whether people in general have ever been able to think in the abstract is arguable, but is is certainly true that a couple of generations ago there were people who were willing to try because this is what education seemed to require and education was a prize to be sought after. The Workers' Educational Association bears witness to the willingness of many non-academics to try to come to grips with the lecture room and the notebook. Preachers could thrive in this atmosphere. Pictures and illustrations may have been used, but they were adjuncts to abstract ideas and explanations of them.

Changes in primary education and the arrival of television have changed all that. No longer do children learn countries by just looking at a map and memorising long lists of what comes from where. Projects, collections and the like give the child an involvement in what he is doing, and learning is a by-product of enjoyment. French is no longer something in a book; it is more likely to be a voice on a tape. Learning how to set up a home and administer your finances is no longer 'being told', but going round the local stores, deciding what you would buy, finding out how much it would cost and learning to balance it with your income. Radio may have been able to deal with the abstract, but television cannot and we live in a television age.

What seems out of this to spell the end of preaching really only spells the beginning of it for the preacher with imagination. He may need to train himself to be something of a cross between a teacher and a TV producer, but if he can the world is waiting. Not many preachers will be able to have a screen over the pulpit where stills could be flashed up to illuminate the discourse, and the use of films as part of the sermon may be completely out, but the use of film material in lieu of part of the sermon ought not to be beyond his grasp, and the tape recorder on which short extracts can be played as part of the sermon, either as introduction or illustration, should certainly be possible. An account of a conversation, or a report of a television play, by the preacher bears no relation to the value of actually hearing the conversation or being reminded of the dialogue. In small congregations, and many congregations are small, the passing round of pictures is easy if only the minister can leave his pulpit and sit among his congregation, and where none of this is possible then the preacher will just have to work all the harder at presenting what he has to say in verbal pictures. The method is certainly no more modern then the days of Jesus, whose parables were straight stories from life, and may even be traced further back to Nathan with his ewe lamb or Isaiah with his vineyard.

If in addition the preacher has the freedom (and Free Church preachers have) to plan the whole service and not just the sermon, then the whole service needs to be brought into the picture. This is more than just picking the hymns and readings which are relevant or remotely connected with the theme. That method assumes a certain basic form that has to be honoured. It is rather a matter of sitting down to see how the total theme can be presented by readings, exposition, interpretation, action and dialogue, perhaps with something of the skill of a television producer. Unless a minister has nothing else to do, and has a few competent people to help him, he just cannot hope to do this twice a Sunday, but judiciously used it is an approach to worship which can send people away longing for more.

Caryl Micklem in his essay has focussed attention on some real problems connected with the Lord's Supper and has pleaded for a de-sacralisation of it. Let us eat it rather than observe it! Let us relate it to the home rather than to the church! And I wouldn't wish to take anything away from his plea. But if we are to continue it in church for the time being (and I have no doubts on this one) then this too needs to be related and made part of the picture. The Lord's Supper is irrelevant in people's minds very often because it is completely unrelated to the rest of the service. It is supposed to stand on its own feet as an isolated event. But why? It is the climax of the church's worship and should arise therefore out of it and be part of it. It is worth noting here, too, Neville Clark's remark that the sacrament cannot be made relevant unless it *is* relevant.

Without at this juncture going into detail as to how this could be achieved, it is a useful exercise for a preacher to begin by deciding to have communion on certain specific festivals. The christian festivals of Easter Day, Whitsunday and Christmas are obvious choices. Let him have it also on Harvest, on Christian Aid Sunday, on Education Sunday and on Mothering Sunday, and let him ask himself how the essence of the Word and the Sacrament can arise out of this theme. At times such relating may stretch his imagination to the limit and he may leave his congregation floundering and thinking that they have never heard it or seen it in that way before, but he will nevertheless be putting both theme and method in a new dimension. He will be breaking right away from 'that which has to be done' and will be engaged instead in exploring a theme.

The mention above of Nathan and the parables serves to pinpoint the third issue. The preacher today must be willing to leave issues open-ended and to let the listener complete the picture.

Once you have a spirit of free enquiry, questioning and even democracy in the primary schools it is not surprising that by the time these youngsters are nineteen they are ready to challenge the places of higher education, and once a nine-year-old is encouraged to test what the teacher says rather than to believe it because the teacher says so and she knows, it is not surprising that adults will reject the kind of preacher who claims, even faintly, to tell them what the faith is or what to do about it. This has often wrongly been interpreted as a rejection of the preacher's message. It is more likely to be rejection of the preacher, or at any rate of his method. There are many people who want all the help the preacher can give them in doing the sums of life; what they do not want him to do is to rush in and give them the answers.

Life is not quite like mathematics where the method of working may vary but all must come to the same answer in the end. Life is so varied that different people may arrive at different answers and interpretations, and there are few things more infuriating when you are working on a problem than the kind of person who looks over your shoulder and tells you what the answer is. It is all the more infuriating because sometimes when you have seen one answer you find it impossible to see any other answers, so that to give the answer prematurely may well be the one way of preventing a person from arriving at what happens to be the right answer for him.

This is not to say that every sermon must be as carefully balanced in its presentation as those radio and television discussions where both sides must be fairly presented and no conclusions reached. A speech or sermon may present one point of view, provided it is clear that it is one point of view, and still raise issues in such a way as to leave the hearer free to draw conclusions different from those of the speaker. Balance may be provided over a period rather than in any particular discourse, for one of the advantages that a preacher has is that he tends to be sure of much the same congregation week after week, and nobody should take it amiss if he seems one week to deny something that he has affirmed the week before. Truth has many facets and one of the virtues of truth is that it can best be expressed by a presentation of opposites.

92

To begin with, a minister's congregation may have some difficulty with this. They may have been trained to believe that what he says is 'gospel' just because he says it, and if what he says is different from what they have always believed they may find a crisis of faith developing. If they try to come to terms with it, only to discover that six months later he is saying something different, then they are liable to conclude that perhaps he doesn't know himself what he believes. But the preacher is also a pastor, and in this capacity he can help his people gradually to see that life is a pilgrimage, that the Christian has to learn to live in a tent, and that when he has just got used to looking at an idea one way he needs to turn his tent round, or move his pitch, and look at it another way. Even the foundations of the faith need this kind of open treatment; much more so is it true of peripheral matters.

This may relate to what was said earlier about the minister's crisis. Part of it is living with this kind of uncertainty, for both minister and member, but it is also this uncertainty that presents the preacher with his most exciting opportunity.

Fourthly, the preacher must be prepared to let the changes in his congregation come over a period of time. If a man tackles preaching along these lines he may well be told that he is not preaching any more for conversion. If he was brought up to believe that preaching for conversion from atheism to faith was the essence of all true preaching then he may have some difficulty at this point. But conversion is not a once-for-all experience; it is a continuing one. I have no doubt that preaching of the kind I have described does bring changes, and often changes far more far-reaching than that which seemed in twenty minutes to bring one man from death to life, though this is not always readily apparent and many people do not even see it in themselves. The wise pastor will learn to spot this and to be thankful. What matters is that the change takes place and has its effect, not that everybody has the satisfaction of rejoicing in it.

It is also possible in this way not simply to change the approach of the individual, but to change the whole life and outlook of a congregation. How long this takes depends on the size and nature of the congregation, but there can be no doubt that it can happen and does.

Five years ago I had my own doubts about preaching and the future of the preaching ministry. I still have, if preaching is to be restricted to two twenty minute discourses expounding pure biblical theology, but if the preacher can begin to apply his theological understanding to the events of life, and if he can vary his method and approach, then these are days of opportunity.

Similarly, if the congregation learns to eat and drink together in the kind of atmosphere and environment and with the kind of relevance that we have envisaged, this too changes the congregation. The Lord's Supper begins to effect the kind of corporate community that we have so often talked about when we have met around the Table, but have so rarely succeeded in achieving, and if you wonder why then go back to Caryl Micklem's essay and re-read now what he says about it. Eating and drinking together will do nothing for the community overnight, but it could do a lot for the community over a decade.

CHURCH STRUCTURES

Plenty here for a man to be depressed about whatever his theological or ecclesiastical bent. One man is depressed because the bells are worn out, the tower unsafe and only piped music possible; another is depressed because his church is wealthy enough to restore both bells and tower and will do so while refusing to give more than a pittance to Christian Aid. One man is depressed because the various church organisations are diminishing in number and his people won't come out any longer to evening meetings; his colleague is depressed because so many people still turn up for what he regards as trivialities whilst rejecting the weightier aspects of the church's mission.

The root of the problem at the present time is the tension between the old and the new, and the more a man tries to cling to the old in a changing situation or to press on to the new in a more reactionary situation the more likely he is to be aware of a crisis in his ministry. What he has to learn to do is to acknowledge the distinction and then allow both to co-exist. Of course it would be better to have all motorways for cars or all country lanes for pony and trap, and many of the problems of driving arise from the necessity to adjust when you pass from quiet country lane to motorway, or from motorway to suburban high road. It would be easier and safer to have one or the other. But we haven't. Possibly we never shall have. Therefore we have to learn to live with both.

If a man does this the possibility is that his people will polarise into progressive and reactionary groupings. Again it would be easier if you could say that all the old people will be among the conservatives and all the students and young people among the progressives. But you can't. There is a stubborn conservatism among many young people who have only known one way of believing or behaving and who fear that if they
94

deviate they are likely to head for disaster. There are older people who have moved around and matured so much that they can constantly adjust to new pressures and respond to new opportunities. Most ministers have just got to learn to recognise both sorts and to respond to both sorts.

The difficulty for the minister whose sympathies are with the radicals may, however, be greater at this point than for the man who is more conservative. The reason is obvious. The conservative minister continues to minister to his flock and the radicals tend to stay away. The progressive minister must always be trying to move somebody. He is acutely aware that he and his people are citizens of no abiding city and must constantly be on the move, so that even when he has won one battle he is immediately conscious of another to be fought so that more land can be possessed, and however radical his congregation may appear to be, he is of necessity failing unless he is urging them forward.

For him, the temptation is to hive off with such radicals as he can find, but, like Ernest Marvin, he soon comes to the conclusion that he couldn't do any better on his own, much less with fellow rebels. In any case, in some denominations this would be impossible; the most a man could hope to do would be to work himself into a church with a strong radical tradition. In baptist and congregational churches with a strong streak of independence it is more of a possibility since there is nothing to stop a radical minister and congregation setting up their own church just as many evangelicals have done. But if a minister reflects on this long enough he will soon come to see the impossibility of it. The real radicals, in fact, just don't want this kind of church structure, and just as their ideal tends to be a church without buildings, so their next ideal is likely to be a church without a minister, or at least without a minister dependent on his congregation for his livelihood. What he must try to do therefore is to keep his nose to the grindstone and work even among his reactionaries until he can help some of them out of their 'straitjacket'. To do this he will have to pay attention to church structure to the extent of shaping it for the future. Situations vary, but in general the minister in crisis may find hope if he can sort out the following points.

First, he can begin to strip down the church to a minimum and give the faithful all the help possible by concentrating on a few necessities. Again, the extent to which a minister is involved in administration varies from denomination to denomination, but the job of the radical is not only to extricate himself as much as possible from administration

95

but also to extricate his members from it also to release them for their mission. To take but one example. Matters of maintenance and fabric in many public buildings are in the hands of one man whose job it is, within an agreed budget, to maintain the fabric in good condition. Too much time in church circles is spent in arguing out each point in a committee and then putting it carefully through boards of deacons, courts of elders, church meetings and parish councils. Many other items of expense are handled on a month to month basis which could just as readily be settled on an annual basis. If a minister is prepared to put in a few years' hard work in one parish along these lines he may save hours of time and effort for himself and for his members in the long run.

Having reduced the inessentials he can then increase the time set apart for mission. Much advantage can be gained here from *ad hoc* groups of people trained for mission, along the lines referred to in the B.C.C. Report (6) where it is suggested that the role of the church is to become an agent for the creation of community groups rather than the focus around which an existing community lives. Ministerial leadership will be needed for their establishment. One group may concentrate on education, another on industry, another on problems of mental health, another on arts and the theatre and one on home and family life. The various sections into which denominational citizenship departments are divided will give any man his starting list. But avoid establishing structures. Avoid the committees, constitutions, appointment of officers, annual general meetings, etc. etc. that have bedevilled so many church organisations over the years, so that the tool can be kept flexible, and be more than ready to take up Caryl Micklem's earlier point about sharing in these common interests and social concerns with all who are concerned and not only with fellow christians. 'Christ in mouth of stranger' is a vital discovery which all of us must learn to make continually. A lot of ministerial time may go on this kind of thing, but will be found to be ultimately rewarding as more and more members begin to move outside the confines of the church structures to fulfil their christian vocation.

Meanwhile much of the traditional church work may continue. It is usually a mistake to try to stop it. Nevertheless, by clearly establishing his own priorities, the minister will soon be seen to be establishing priorities for the church.

Secondly, in consultation with his church officers, he can begin to question locally the idea of one minister/one church. It is still too readily assumed that every church should have its own full-time

96

minister and that any departure from this is a second-rate substitute. It is further too readily assumed that if a church can afford an assistant or associate minister then it is a sign of growth or success. What is needed in the case of the church is something akin to what is happening in the medical profession at the level of the G.P. The single-handed practice is rapidly giving place to effective teams with a multiplicity of skills, and is not solely a move to ease the lot of the doctor.

In the church almost all the experiments that have taken place so far have been within a single denomination. Such experiments are not necessarily successful and may even be a positive hindrance. Five ministers of one denomination working as a team in a town of 100,000 may effectively prevent each of them from working with his nearest counterpart. Geography here is more important than denominational confessions, and minister and people should now begin to plan for some united policy with all Christians in their locality. The women's meetings in each of these churches, together with the men's fellowships and the youth groups, all serviced by their own ministers, must now give place to single groups for matters of education, industry, theatre, etc., and all serviced by one of the local ministers working in a team. Thamesmead may begin to set the pattern and just because it is pioneering, will show up the mistakes that can be made when trying to do this in a new-town area. More effort must be made to discover the snags when pioneering along these lines is done in an old-town area, and that gives plenty of scope for us all.

Thirdly, churches may begin to think out how far they need full-time and how far they need part-time ministers. The Baptists have given much thought to this and their report, *Ministry Today and Tomorrow*, has run into trouble because the news got around that the denomination was planning to reduce the number of ministers from 1,200 to 400 over a period of years. In fact, this was not the case. What was being said was that the number of ministers was reducing itself and that the denomination should begin to plan for this reduction. The Paul Report met with a similar reception a few years ago when it pointed out that many of the anglican clergy were located in the country when they were much more needed in the towns.

Possibly in both cases the wrong point has been taken up. The issue is not that the church can no longer afford or provide so many full-time ministers and must therefore learn to do with less. It is rather a positive point. Do we in our present situation need full-time men or part-time men?

One answer is that we certainly do still need men who can give their whole time and individual attention to the work of the church and particularly to her mission; we don't in fact have to choose between Caryl Micklem and Neville Clark at this point, though we do have to determine more closely just what we mean by a full-time fully trained minister and we may need to clarify just what he does. Once we have done that we may well find that we need them as much if not more than ever we did, and to hold their own in society they will need to be extraordinarily well trained. But it can also be argued that we need an increasing body of people, men and women, who are fully committed to the church's ministry as well as committed to their daily profession or vocation. They need not administer word and sacrament. They are ministers of a different sort, modern missionaries in secular society, but they are the right arm of the church and can rely on the support of the church in the work they are doing, added to which they will have a special relationship with those full-time ministers who oversee the whole of the church's work. The baptist suggestion of calling them 'supplementary ministers' was not a bad one, so long as this did not give the idea that the essential ministry was the full-time one and the other was only secondary or derivative.

There are not many signs that this kind of thing is happening, though there is encouragement and hope in the fact that it is increasingly being talked about.

Fourthly, there is a need to examine afresh in our time the whole use of buildings. Let it be taken for granted that if we are to have new buildings they should be functional, and let the test of church architecture for the 70's be not 'what should a church (or church hall) look like?' but 'what is it going to have to do?' The radical challenge compels us to go further and ask whether we need the buildings we have got or whether they are a liability to us.

The answer to this question may vary from place to place but the minister who has his eye on the 80's will think twice before he gets involved in any major building schemes. They may be right and necessary, but he will need to start with the assumption that they are not until they can be justified, rather than start with the assumption that they are and that people must therefore be persuaded to give for the construction.

The rest of us would do well to look at what we have and to begin to ask questions. If it is clear that they are old and a drain on our resources, or that they are of the wrong kind for the work we have to
98

do, then consideration must be given to altering them or to replacing them. At the same time all this is likely to be a costly business and many of them will yield very little if their site is sold, so that for most churches the immediate issue is simply that of making maximum use of what is there, remembering that in many communities the church is the only body that can supply the premises that the community needs. This in itself may be part of our mission and is a challenge to a minister and congregation to see what can be done with a difficult situation.

The real challenge of church buildings, however, is a much larger one, for it cannot be tackled by one church or congregation in isolation from all the others. Imagine a business with fifty branches in a town of 100,000, all the branches of similar construction and design. Business is not exactly booming and even if it were the nature of the operation has changed somewhat over the last couple of decades. The centres of population have also changed. Somebody needs to sit down and plan a whole strategy. Put like that, the challenge to church and ministry in our day is obvious.

Immediately the objection will be raised. Many of the branches are tied by ancient trusts and denominational allegiances. This is not an objection. It is a challenge, and a very big challenge. If Ernest Marvin is right (and I have no doubt on this point) that we need more people working from fewer bases and if I am right (and I have no doubt on this one either) that many of our buildings are either in the wrong place or of the wrong kind for what we now want to do, or both, then lots of buildings have to be sold and a few, well-planned, well-appointed buildings have to go up. We have the resources within the church, but it isn't always possible to make use of those resources. Recent legislation for shared use of church premises has been a start and is on the right lines. What is needed next is legislation which will enable Baptists to sell their property in one place and invest it in property of an ecumenical nature or even of another denomination in another place. We are all part of the church of Jesus Christ and the resources need to be pooled. We need the kind of legislation which will enable a thriving baptist church to sell its capital resources and put them into a united scheme where the work can be more effectively carried on. How long it would take such legislation to be passed is anybody's guess but it certainly isn't too soon to begin.

Another objection is that in the case of a business once the management decides on a policy the staff have to fit in, whereas in the church the 'staff' (i.e. members) have voting power. This is not an

99

objection either, though it may be a problem, but church people are not so rigid or so stupid that they cannot come to see what is right and necessary if the lead is clear and strong and backed by sound argument.

The issue here is not only one of economics, trusts or denominational affiliation. It is one of attitude. The time to begin to create the right attitude is now—if not before! The radical minister who senses a crisis in his ministry has here a golden opportunity to begin to plan for the rest of the twentieth century.

PERSONAL TIME AND FREEDOM

If the problem for the young minister is how to be loyal to the dictates of his conscience when his church members expect something different from him, the problem for the older man is how to adjust to the demands of the contemporary situation when his training and background have all left him with certain presuppositions. He was brought up to believe, for example that he should spend mornings in his study, afternoons visiting and evenings down at the church. Or he was trained to appear in church at fixed hours for morning and evening prayer and to spend the rest of his time walking round the parish. Now he knows that many of the meetings he is called upon to attend are unproductive, some are unnecessary and a few are a positive hindrance to the church's mission. Working wives plus television and do-it-yourself make casual calling almost impossible compared with the more leisurely days of the thirties. A reading of Bonhoeffer may have given a man the feeling that he does not want to minister to people only at times of personal crisis. How then can he re-design his whole ministry to meet the current demands and still be happy in his conscience?

What he has to do is to settle for himself what is his essential and effective ministry, and first commit himself to these things. If he has time left over, then on the principle that his time is his own, under God, to use as seems to him to be vital, he will pick out what needs to be done in the community, and may not worry too much what he does qua minister and what he does qua layman. Precise details again will vary from man to man and all I can do is to set down what seems to me to be the most vital and hopeful.

One prime duty of both preachers and pastors, for example, is helping people to see the significance of what they are doing and of what they are looking at. The nature of the christian vocation within work, social and family life has still not been appreciated by many people, who see life as one thing and christian witness or service as
100

something added on to it.

One woman on a new housing estate, for instance, complained to her minister that she found so little time for christian work. Before she married she had constantly been at work in the church, but now with a husband on shift work and two young children there was so little opportunity. It needed a sympathetic minister to explain to her that her christian work was in caring for her husband and in training her children, and what better field of service could she wish for. Like the man who had been speaking prose all his life without knowing it she was fully committed. It just needed somebody to point it out to her.

There there was the teacher who was asked about christian witness within his profession and immediately started to talk about all his extra-curricular activities. When pressed to his school life he went on about R.E. and the school assembly. It needed a pastor to show him that perhaps his greatest witness was in the personal relationships he had with the children, with parents and with other members of staff, as well as with the quality of his workmanship.

If parents and teachers find it difficult to see what they are doing, how much more the man on the factory floor, the lorry driver, the stock broker, etc. etc. There are many ways of achieving this and door to door pastoral visitation is not the only one. A minister, for instance, may hold regular group discussion in his own home to which his people may come in their own categories or in groups which cross the frontiers. A weekly meeting like this, perhaps taking different groups each week, may contribute far more to the kingdom than a straight devotional address to the mid-week service or prayer meeting or a nightly attendance at evensong. Neither should it be said that such a man is neglecting prayer, for prayer is engagement with the depths of life and with the mystery of life, and there might well be much more such engagement in this kind of group than in the traditional service or prayer meeting. Another way is for a minister to set aside two or three evenings a week simply for social entertaining in his own home as once he set aside two or three afternoons for calling on houses. Let people just come and talk. It may be a long time before anything seems to happen, but if the minister knows the situation his people live in, knows what is going on around him, and knows his theology then he can have a whale of a time interpreting this for people in practical terms and relating it to their daily life, and they will love him for it.

There there is a field of opportunity for helping people pastorally and with no strings attached. It is true that many people are afraid of approaching the minister because they think he will get at them, and it is equally true that many professional social workers mistrust the minister for the same reason. Nevertheless if a man is prepared to work patiently at building up relationships confidence can be established and in so doing he will not only be finding a useful niche for himself but he will also be helping to redeem the church in the eyes of those who care for people. Similarly if he can listen with what are popularly called non-judgmental attitudes, he may soon find that the whole community is beating a pathway to his front door, and in spite of the wonderful social services and the breadth of the voluntary organisations there is still need in most communities for one man who is able by the very nature of his position to stand outside it all and occasionally to interpret or build bridges.

If a man is alert, and if he keeps clearly in mind the mission of the church, he will then find a dual role in the community. On the one hand he is in a key position to initiate new programmes of caring or education. There are many things which both voluntary and statutory bodies would like to see done, but which they are unable to initiate either because they have no money, no man-power or no premises. A minister who cares, backed by a church who cares, has here a unique opportunity. The minister is the one free person in the community able to adjust his time if he wills. His church may not be wealthy, but if they wish they can raise the money that is needed. Often they are the one body with premises unused for many hours of the day. It may only be a temporary activity. The new 'thing' once established may go off on its own. This doesn't matter. The work has been done and there is new territory to be explored.

On the other hand, the minister is often able to play a reconciliatory role between various bodies engaged in a similar fuction but not always working together. Sometimes there is an unhelpful division between health and welfare services, sometimes between town and county services; in the case of schools there may be local rivalries and the integration of the social services just at the present time is bound to cause some heart-searchings. A minister who is able to move freely on both sides, who may even have members or at least contacts on both sides, can do a lot of useful work by inviting both to meet in his home with no axes to grind and no ramparts to be defended. Good personal relationships are often the first step towards improved services.

In most communities there are bodies in need of leadership or voluntary services. The Samaritan movement usually relies on good

102

clerical leadership and unless the churches are prepared to set their ministers apart for this work it may not be done. Marriage Guidance Councils have similar requirements. Local radio, often run on a shoe-string, needs men of ministerial vision, ability and stature to assist in some of its programmes, and in a day when so many people are heavily committed to their professions the minister has a useful and vital field of service.

The achievement of all this is not without its difficulties. Obviously no man can fulfil all these roles. What is crucial is that he learns to map out the territory where he will fight and where his gifts will be most fully used, and get on with it.

Some churches will react against all this. There is still the feeling in too many churches that the minister belongs to the church and so-called 'outside' demands on his time and energy will be resented. The minister's last consolation is that he is there as the servant of God and not as the servant of the church, and if he is willing to educate his people, and to try to show them that what he is doing is a worthwhile and a necessary job that he feels called to fulfil he will be very unlucky indeed if he cannot find some members of his congregation who are willing to back him. Then, with a cool head and a clear mind, with the courage to act on his own and with patience to live through the trials and turmoils until he is vindicated, he will succeed, and it will not be long before he is no longer alone in the field, but is actually backed by a congregation all ready to follow his lead.

Let nobody underestimate the crisis for the ministry at the present time, but let it be equally clear that for the right man crisis is nothing more than opportunity.

1. It is also worth noting that the nature of theology itself has changed in the last decade. It is no longer a coherent system of belief, but rather a process of exploration. The theologian has been described by Kenneth Grayston as an explorer travelling in unfamiliar country. (Steven G. Mackie, *Patterns of Ministry,* pp 72-73, 86.Cf. *The Shape of the Ministry,* 3.)
2. David L. Edwards (ed), *Preparing for the Ministry of the 1970's* pp 122-123.
3. *The Shape of the Ministry,* 29.
4. C.U.P., especially pp 207-8.
5. Printed in New Christian, November 1967.
6. *The Shape of the Ministry,* 5.